THE
VERY BEST,
HANDS-ON,
KINDA DANGEROUS
FAMILY
DEVOTIONS

Volume 3

THE VERY BEST, HANDS-ON, KINDA DANGEROUS FAMILY DEVOTIONS

52 ACTIVITIES YOUR KIDS WILL NEVER FORGET

Volume 3

TIM SHOEMAKER

Revell

a division of Baker Publishing Group
Grand Rapids, Michigan

© 2024 by Tim Shoemaker

Published by Revell
a division of Baker Publishing Group
Grand Rapids, Michigan
RevellBooks.com

Printed in the United States of America

Library of Congress Cataloging-in-Publication Data
Names: Shoemaker, Tim, author.
Title: The very best, hands-on, kinda dangerous family devotions : 52 activities your kids will
    never forget / Tim Shoemaker.
Description: Grand Rapids : Baker Publishing Group, 2019.
Identifiers: LCCN 2018045152 | ISBN 9780800744908 (pbk.)
Subjects: LCSH: Christian education—Home training. | Christian education of children. |
    Object-teaching. | Families—Religious life.
Classification: LCC BV1590 .S56 2019 | DDC 249—dc23
LC record available at https://lccn.loc.gov/2018045152

All activities and projects in this book are intended to be performed under adult supervision. Appropriate and reasonable caution is required at all times, and the suggested activities cannot replace common sense and sound judgment. Observe safety and caution at all times. The author and publisher disclaim all liability for any damage, mishap, or injury that may occur from engaging in the activities featured in this book.

The author is represented by the Cyle Young Literary Elite agency.

Baker Publishing Group publications use paper produced from sustainable forestry practices and post-consumer waste whenever possible.

24 25 26 27 28 29 30   7 6 5 4 3 2 1

Dedicated to my dad, Vaughn Richard Shoemaker.
The thing I remember most about family devotions
was his dedication to keeping at it—even though he probably
wasn't seeing results at the time. He had enough faith
to know it was important . . . believing that somehow
it would make a difference.

It did.

Dad demonstrated that a man who loves the Lord
does many things for his family, and teaching his kids
about God is one of them.
My dad massively influenced my life . . . and his legacy lives on.

Call to me and I will answer you and tell you great and unsearchable things you do not know.

Jeremiah 33:3

Fix these words of mine in your hearts and minds; tie them as symbols on your hands and bind them on your foreheads. Teach them to your children, talking about them when you sit at home and when you walk along the road, when you lie down and when you get up.

Deuteronomy 11:18–19

They are not just idle words for you—
they are your life.

Deuteronomy 32:47

CONTENTS

OBJECT LESSONS AND ACTIVITIES

1. Smashed Tomatoes   25

THEME: Low self-esteem / anxiety / hopelessness / realizing God can make much good come from messed-up lives.

We'll smash tomatoes to show how God can make great things happen for us . . . even if our life seems like junk or a total mess.

2. Target Practice   29 ⚠️

THEME: Becoming the kind of person God wants us to be requires aiming on our part.

We'll have the kids aim at a target—blindfolded—to show how we must keep our eyes on the goal if we really want to hit it.

3. Baby Stuff   34

THEME: The need to mature as Christians.

A tricycle race will make the point that failing to mature as Christians limits us and the things we'll be able to do.

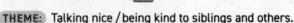

A Quick Key for Parents

 Activities with this symbol are a little more on the dangerous side and will require some extra caution on your part. Additional safety tips and reminders are also included in these lessons.

THIS ISN'T AS HARD AS YOU THINK

I'm so happy you've picked up this book. Before we get started, here's four quick things that will make leading family devotions even easier.

1. There is no particular order you need to stay in here. Scan the table of contents. Find a devotional that looks like it will work for your family this week and go for it. Just jot the date in the margin so you'll know you've done it before. And make the first one you choose to do with your family short and fun.

2. Keep the teaching time short. Often five minutes is all you need after the activity or object lesson is done. If you don't abuse the time factor, the kids won't dread family devotions.

3. Don't try to memorize the lesson for the week. It will only frustrate you because it will be too hard to prepare for the lesson—and then you'll start skipping weeks. It's okay to have the book in front of you when you're teaching the lesson. I always have notes when I'm teaching kids. But my advice? Mark the pages up a bit. Highlight things you want to cover. Make a note in the margin here or there. Cross out things you don't think apply. The kids will see you took the time to study the lesson in advance, and that tells them you think it's really important.

4. Have fun with these. Sure, learning about God is serious business, but there's nothing wrong with the kids thinking that learning about God can be fun. If they are messing around, just roll with it. Relax. Enjoy the time. If you're having fun, the kids will find that family devotions are fun for them too. Keep this up, and you'll see how God uses his truth in your family in wonderful ways.

And for what it's worth? I'm proud of you. Keep going . . . and know that I'm cheering you on!

Tim

LEADING FAMILY DEVOTIONS WILL BE DIFFERENT THIS TIME

Our kids need spiritual training, reinforcement, and modeling at home, but sometimes dads struggle with that. Why? Often it boils down to one or more of a handful of reasons.

1. Men fear their kids won't really listen. Some guys have sat in too many boring devotionals themselves. They imagine the kids will be messing around or bored—and they'll have no way to maintain control. That's downright embarrassing to a man.

2. Men fear they're not qualified in some way. Some guys feel inadequate—like they should know the Bible better. What if they're asked a question they can't answer?

3. Men fear they've disqualified themselves somehow. Maybe the enemy reminds some guys of their sin and failures in the past. *Who am I to teach the kids?* they think. *I'd be a hypocrite. I know what I've done . . . or am still doing.*

4. Men fear they'll fail at having any kind of meaningful family devotions time with the kids. Some guys are sure the kids won't listen, and that this will end with a massive loss on the Dad scoreboard. They may figure that they can't lose if they don't play.

Men often feel like responsibility for family devotions is being dumped on them. Consequently, they feel it's easier not to start than to begin and fail—which is exactly what they believe will happen. This is why pushing and prodding men rarely works. Not for long, anyway.

Let me give you three reasons to be encouraged that *this* time it will be different.

1. Men are wired to protect their kids. Once we realize family devotions are all about protecting our kids from the enemy of our souls, we're more open to the idea of family devotions. Sure, the enemy may tell a dad he's disqualified himself, but that's pretty much trash talk designed to keep a dad from protecting his kids. Once a man gets that, it will be easier for him to get in the ring and fight . . . and to keep going.

2. These devotions will work. They're not Bible studies. Our goal is to simply get one nugget of truth to the kids per lesson. And with active, object lesson openers to each devotional, the kids will stay engaged, not get bored. Every time we'll have an activity right up front, followed by a short nugget of truth. The activity—along with the biblical truth behind it—becomes etched in the minds of our kids.

3. Dad doesn't have to do this alone. Sometimes the best way to do family devotions is for both parents to be involved. Perhaps Dad runs the activity, and then Mom ties in the nugget of truth—or vice versa. This way each parent can work well within their comfort zone. And what do the kids see? Dad and Mom working together to teach spiritual truth. There's nothing wrong with that. The whole responsibility doesn't rest on Dad's shoulders alone.

So, give this a shot. This time it will work—and it will keep working. And let me say something really, really important: have fun with this! Loosen up. Lighten up. Your objective is to have a good time with the activity and tie a simple nugget of truth in at the end. Do this and you'll enjoy the devotionals, and the kids will too. And most importantly, they'll remember the nuggets of truth too, which are all about helping and protecting them spiritually.

You can do this!

Smashed Tomatoes

THEME: Low self-esteem / anxiety / hopelessness / realizing God can make much good come from messed-up lives.

THINGS YOU'LL NEED

- ☐ Tomatoes . . . nice big ripe ones, one for each member of the family
- ☐ Resealable plastic bags, gallon size, one or two bags per member of the family
- ☐ Rubber mallet (optional)

Advance Prep

There's no real prep needed, other than to pick up the supplies and decide if you're going to do this indoors or outdoors. Also, this lesson can be even more effective if you choose a meal for the family today that contains smashed tomatoes in the ingredients. Spaghetti. Lasagna. Chili. Pizza. Or any food your kids might like where they'd add ketchup or salsa. Adding the meal is optional, but it may help reinforce the truth of this lesson.

And let me say one more thing: you've picked a great devotional here. The nugget of truth your kids will get? Absolutely essential. Google "teenage girls and suicide." It will break your heart. But you'll also see why this lesson is so important. Sometimes kids do desperate things when they feel like junk. They become anxious. Fearful. Hopeless. That is where you can help them tremendously by sharing the truth of this lesson. When our sons or daughters feel like junk, they need to remember how God makes great things out of messed-up lives. And you're going to help them remember that truth—by smashing tomatoes.

Running the Activity

Give each of the kids a big, juicy tomato, and tell them you'd like them to smash it. You may want them to throw the tomatoes in the air so that they splat on the driveway. Or you may want to put each tomato in a resealable plastic bag. With this method, the kids can use a rubber mallet to pummel that tomato or use their fists to give it a good pounding.

When the tomato is nicely smashed, you're ready to move on. If you smashed the tomatoes on the driveway, pick up the biggest chunks and drop them in a clear plastic bag so you can hold it up easily. If you smashed the tomatoes inside plastic bags to begin with, you're all set.

Teaching the Lesson

Hold up a plastic bag filled with smashed tomatoes and ask these questions:

What do we do with smashed tomatoes?

Do we throw them out?

Are they junk?

Some kids may think the tomatoes are junk, others may realize they're not. Either answer works; just move on.

These smashed tomatoes may *look* like junk, but in the hands of a chef or cook, they're just the beginning of many things you really like. Can anybody name some? (For example: pizza, spaghetti, lasagna, salsa, chili, ketchup.)

There are times in life when we will feel like junk. Maybe we feel we're not the prettiest or most handsome or we're not exactly popular, talented, athletic, smart, or whatever. And sometimes we can feel like junk when we really mess up in some way.

Do you know what I want you to remember when you feel like junk? God is like a heavenly chef who makes great things from messed-up lives.

Remember the story of Moses? *If your kids know it, just hit the main points of the account starting in Exodus 2.*

- Moses was in a position to help his people, but he messed up and killed an Egyptian.
- What do you think Moses felt like when he was on the run in the desert? I'd guess he felt like junk. Like a smashed tomato. He probably thought he'd never get another chance to help his people.
- But God didn't want Moses to use his position simply to help his people. God had a much bigger plan. He wanted Moses to set his people free.
- God turned that smashed tomato of a man into one of the greatest leaders of all time.

Summing It Up

Just like we need to smash tomatoes to make some of our favorite meals, sometimes we need to go through hard things so that we learn to trust God . . . so that we become the person he wants us to be.

> For we are God's handiwork, created in Christ Jesus to do good works, which God prepared in advance for us to do. (Eph. 2:10)

God has a plan for us, and he's there to help us get there.

Remember, there will be many, many times you'll feel like junk. That is part of life. When that happens, it may feel like your world has ended. But I want you to remember the point of this smashed tomato lesson: God is like a heavenly chef. He makes great things out of messed-up lives. Bring your mess or your concern to him and ask him to make something of it. Ask him to make you into the person he desires, so that you can do the things he's prepared for you to do. God loves prayers like that. When you feel like junk, give it to God and trust him to work things out in great ways!

If you plan to have pizza, spaghetti, lasagna, or another tomato-based meal with the kids, this would be a great time to tie that in too.

Target Practice

THEME: Becoming the kind of person God wants us to be requires aiming on our part.

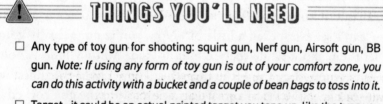

THINGS YOU'LL NEED

- ☐ Any type of toy gun for shooting: squirt gun, Nerf gun, Airsoft gun, BB gun. *Note: If using any form of toy gun is out of your comfort zone, you can do this activity with a bucket and a couple of bean bags to toss into it.*

- ☐ Target—it could be an actual printed target you tape up, like the type you get at a sporting goods store, or it could just be a bull's-eye you draw on a piece of paper. Note: If you choose a squirt gun, it may be more fun to use a lit candle for the target. If you choose a BB gun, you may want to choose a plastic milk carton filled with water for the target. The BB will cause it to spring a leak, which just makes it that much more fun to hit.

- ☐ Safety glasses for each of the kids—and for every adult present. These are essential if you are shooting any type of gun.

- ☐ Blindfold—a scarf works fine for this.

Advance Prep

Picking up the toy gun is the big task for prep. If you're using some form of Airsoft or BB gun, I'm assuming you'll find a safe place to do this outside. I hope I don't need to say this, but be sure to place the target where there's no risk of a stray shot hurting property or people, okay?

If you're using the bean bag and bucket method, this activity can easily be done indoors.

Running the Activity

Have each of the kids take a turn hitting the target. Either they're shooting at the target or they're tossing the bean bags into the bucket if you preferred to keep toy guns out of this. To keep things simpler, from this point on, I'm going to assume you've chosen to have the kids shoot some form of toy gun.

After each has had their turn, you're going to go through the lineup again. But this time, you'll put a blindfold on your shooter. Make sure they can't see—not even a little bit. Now, you're not actually going to let them shoot while they're blindfolded. All they'll do is point the gun where they think the target is. They'll hold the unloaded gun—but keep the safety on. We also don't want the gun cocked or their finger on the trigger, just to be safe.

Turn them several times to disorient them a bit. And here's a sneaky tip: you'll want to move slightly yourself, at a slower speed, so that when you stop turning them you're in a different spot as well. If they orient their aim based on the location of your voice and don't realize you were moving as well, their aim will definitely be off, which is what you want.

Once you stop spinning them, ask them to keep their finger off the trigger and point the gun where they think the target is. (In the case of the bucket and beanbag method, you can go ahead and let them toss the bean bag). Unless they're peeking somehow, their aim will almost certainly be off—which is exactly what you want.

Now, tell them to freeze in that position, and remove their blindfold so they can see how they did. Likely they aren't nearly as close to the target as they were the first time when they weren't wearing the blindfold. Perfect! You're ready to transition to a spiritual truth.

Teaching the Lesson

The key to hitting a target is what?

- Aiming. Keeping the target in our sights.
- Unless we keep our eyes on the target, we likely won't hit it.

The same principle applies to life. There are some "targets" God would like us to hit. Hitting those targets will take some careful aiming—just like hitting a paper target with the toy gun.

What types of targets does God want us to hit?

Doesn't he want us to aim to be more like Jesus? What might that look like?

- Loving others and caring for them like Jesus does.
- Forgiving others like Jesus does.
- Helping others like Jesus does.
- Being honest, dependable, and trustworthy like Jesus is.
- Being humble like Jesus is.

We could add plenty to that list. But if we don't aim—if we don't keep our eyes on Jesus—we won't hit the target. Our aim will be off. We won't become the person God desires us to be.

Summing It Up

Here's some Bible verses to consider.

> How can a young person stay on the path of purity?
>> By living according to your word.
> I seek you with all my heart;
>> do not let me stray from your commands. (Ps. 119:9–10)

Therefore, holy brothers and sisters, who share in the heavenly calling, fix your thoughts on Jesus, whom we acknowledge as our apostle and high priest. (Heb. 3:1)

Therefore, since we are surrounded by such a great cloud of witnesses, let us throw off everything that hinders and the sin that so easily entangles. And let us run with perseverance the race marked out for us, fixing our eyes on Jesus, the pioneer and perfecter of faith. For the joy set before him he endured the cross, scorning its shame, and sat down at the right hand of the throne of God. Consider him who endured such opposition from sinners, so that you will not grow weary and lose heart. (12:1–3)

The key isn't simply reading the verses. We need to put them into practice. If we want to hit a target, we actually need to pull the trigger and do what God's Word tells us to do. That is the whole point of what Jesus is saying in Matthew 7:24–27:

Therefore everyone who hears these words of mine and puts them into practice is like a wise man who built his house on the rock. The rain came down, the streams rose, and the winds blew and beat against that house; yet it did not fall, because it had its foundation on the rock. But everyone who hears these words of mine and does not put them into practice is like a foolish man who built his house on sand. The rain came down, the streams rose, and the winds blew and beat against that house, and it fell with a great crash.

One last thought. We all want to become the person God desires us to be—with his help—don't we? There's a story in 2 Chronicles that tells about King Rehoboam (Ray-ha-BOW-um), who was King Solomon's son. Check out this verse:

He did evil because he had not set his heart on seeking the LORD. (2 Chron. 12:14)

King Rehoboam didn't set his aim, didn't direct his heart to seek the Lord. And because he didn't, he messed up. Keeping our eyes on Jesus isn't just about physically aiming, right? It's about setting our hearts in the right direction. Having a heart—a desire—to become the person God intends each of us to be. Unless we take aim at that, we'll miss the mark. And even more tragic? We'll likely do bad things—evil things—if we aren't careful to aim at being the person God wants us to be. King Rehoboam learned that the hard way.

Thankfully, God included Rehoboam's story in the Bible. We can learn from that king's mistake . . . so we never have to make the same one ourselves!

Baby Stuff

THEME: The need to mature as Christians.

THINGS YOU'LL NEED

☐ Tricycle or similar bike for toddlers. It would be great to have two so the kids can race, but if you can only find one, that will work. You want something here that is much too small for your kids to ride comfortably or easily. You want the trike to actually slow them down because they're too big for it.

☐ Baby prize. For the winner, get something from the infant aisle at the store, such as a disgusting flavor of baby food, a pacifier, or a teething ring. Really, all you need is any baby item your kids would *not* be proud to win.

Advance Prep

Picking up the supplies is all you'll need to do. The tricycle should be something your kids can sit on but are clearly too big to pedal with any efficiency. The idea here is to find a tricycle, Big Wheel, or similar wheeled toy for young kids.

Remember, you can ask around and likely borrow all you need from friends, family, or even from grandparents at your church who have young grandkids in their family.

Running the Activity

Decide on the course you'd like your tricycle-riding contestants to pedal. If you have two trikes, you'll want two of your kids to race each other. If you have one bike (or one child), have them bike the course for time.

The bigger your kids are, the harder time they'll have pedaling that trike. That's perfect. Have the kids each get a turn and record their times.

Teaching the Lesson

A tricycle may be a great thing for a toddler. When they first learned to pedal, a trike was a big deal! It allowed them to go places— faster—than they could on foot. It opened a new world to them in some ways.

But what if some toddler decided to stay with their trike—even as they got older and bigger? The tricycle would slow them down. It would limit them. The fact is, that little tricycle was never intended to be used by someone older.

Can you imagine someone insisting on sticking with their tricycle, even when they did get older? Can you imagine that person pedaling it to high school—and locking it on the bike rack next to real bikes? Can you imagine them pedaling that trike to an after-school job? Ridiculous, right?

It's the same thing with the Christian life. Sure, at some point every Christian is a baby Christian, but God doesn't want us to stay there. He wants us to grow and mature.

What are some ways Christians might still be acting like babies instead of maturing?

- Babies are selfish. It's all about what they want. *Wah, wah, wah.* They're all about making sure their needs are met. Maturing means we are looking out for others—putting their needs first.

  Do nothing out of selfish ambition or vain conceit. Rather, in humility value others above yourselves, not looking to your own interests but each of you to the interests of the others. (Phil. 2:3–4)

- Babies or young kids are often ungrateful. They expect people to bend over backward for them. Mature Christians are more grateful to God and others.

- Babies make lots of messes that others around them need to clean up. Maturing Christians aren't making the same messes over and over again.

- Babies can't feed themselves. Mature Christians aren't completely dependent on a pastor feeding them. They know how to go to the Word and feed themselves.

  Do your best to present yourself to God as one approved, a worker who does not need to be ashamed and who correctly handles the word of truth. (2 Tim. 2:15)

- Babies don't make terrific decisions. Caretakers have to keep an eye on them so they don't hurt themselves and must be careful to protect them from danger—because babies will wander out into the street, or worse, if left unattended. Maturing Christians learn to avoid dangers and the traps that can cause them harm. They learn how to consider God and follow his leading when they're in the process of making decisions.

> Trust in the LORD with all your heart
> and lean not on your own understanding;
> in all your ways submit to him,
> and he will make your paths straight. (Prov. 3:5–6)

You could keep brainstorming this topic with the kids, but by this time, they see how important it is to mature as a Christian. Good job. Now it's time to move on.

Summing It Up

The kid who won't give up their trike is going to be more and more limited the older they get. They won't be able to go places they might have gone if they had their driver's license and a car.

If we don't mature as Christians, we'll limit ourselves from experiencing so much that God has planned for us. We'll lose out. And often we'll find ourselves in messes or trouble or danger.

It seems to me that "growing up" as a Christian is a really good thing, and something we can ask God to help us do.

I have this prize for the winner of our little race. *Now is the time to award that baby food, teething ring, or whatever it is you bought.*

This isn't a very satisfying award, is it? And kids, I can tell you it is the same way in life. A more age appropriate award would have been so much more appreciated, wouldn't it? It's the same with our Christian life. There are rewards to maturing. Things like peace. Love. Joy. Self-control. Kindness. A good reputation. Earning the respect of others. We could go on and on. If we don't mature as Christians, we'll miss out on so many good things. We'll limit ourselves. Like that prize you got, the types of rewards we might get if we don't mature as Christians won't be very satisfying at all.

Human Dartboard

THEME: Talking nice / being kind to siblings and others.

THINGS YOU'LL NEED

- ☐ A close-up headshot photo of each of the kids who will be present for the devotional. Something printed on regular 8.5 x 11 paper is fine. Keep in mind that the pictures will be destroyed.
- ☐ Tacks or tape to affix the photo to your dartboard
- ☐ Darts—ideally, you'll want the nice, sharp ones. Yes, they may be more dangerous, but your kids will get the point (pardon the pun) better than if you use a "safer" dart choice. And you need a dart that will make a hole in the paper you'll tack to the dartboard.
- ☐ Dartboard—a traditional one is great. But if you can't get your hands on one, you can also use a scrap of plywood or foamboard.
- ☐ Safety glasses for every person present, including you. Hey, when kids are throwing darts, safety glasses are a good idea, don't you think?

Advance Prep

The biggest thing to do in advance is to get pictures of the kids. Take individual shots of each of them. Zoom in to get a nice, tight headshot. All you need is their face. And it will definitely be more fun if you ask the kids to make a goofy face for the photo. Now print each picture on 8.5 x 11 paper and have them ready for the family devotional time. You'll also want to find a place to hang the dartboard where a wild throw won't damage anything.

Running the Activity

Be sure everyone is wearing safety glasses. Give each of the kids a turn at throwing darts at the dartboard—without any pictures visible.

Next, tack one or more of the pictures to the dartboard and give each of the kids a chance to throw darts again. This time, likely you'll see a whole lot more enthusiasm. Your kids will probably take careful aim—hoping to land a dart in the face of one of their siblings. For the purpose of teaching this lesson, that will work perfectly. You're ready to move on.

Teaching the Lesson

Okay, that was fun, right? Tell me, which did you enjoy throwing darts at most: the plain dartboard or the pictures?

This is how it can be in life too. We can actually enjoy taking shots at our brothers or sisters—or others. Sometimes we really like taking jabs at them. Maybe we say something nasty. Or we're extra critical of them. Or maybe we just treat them mean or rude in some way.

Of course, we all get that. Sometimes those closest to us can get on our nerves. But as followers of Christ, we have to ask ourselves if that is what Jesus really wants us to do. Let's look at a few Bible verses. *I put a bunch of them here, so just pick the ones you feel will work best with your family.*

You have heard that it was said to the people long ago, "You shall not murder, and anyone who murders will be subject to judgment." But I tell you that anyone who is angry with a brother or sister will be subject to judgment. (Matt. 5:21–22)

Anyone who claims to be in the light but hates a brother or sister is still in the darkness. Anyone who loves their brother and sister lives in the light, and there is nothing in them to make them stumble. But anyone who hates a brother or sister is in the darkness and walks around in the darkness. They do not know where they are going, because the darkness has blinded them. (1 John 2:9–11)

Love is patient, love is kind. It does not envy, it does not boast, it is not proud. It does not dishonor others, it is not self-seeking, it is not easily angered, it keeps no record of wrongs. Love does not delight in evil but rejoices with the truth. It always protects, always trusts, always hopes, always perseveres. (1 Cor. 13:4–7)

This is how we know what love is: Jesus Christ laid down his life for us. And we ought to lay down our lives for our brothers and sisters. (1 John 3:16)

Do not let any unwholesome talk come out of your mouths, but only what is helpful for building others up according to their needs, that it may benefit those who listen. And do not grieve the Holy Spirit of God, with whom you were sealed for the day of redemption. Get rid of all bitterness, rage and anger, brawling and slander, along with every form of malice. Be kind and compassionate to one another, forgiving each other, just as in Christ God forgave you. (Eph. 4:29–32)

Summing It Up

It's easy to give those verbal "digs" to those we know really well, like a brother or sister. Sometimes we really enjoy it too. We know their weak points. We know how to press their buttons. We can hit with a comment or criticism that is sarcastic and hurtful and rude. It isn't kind or spoken in love at all. The truth is, we can get pretty good at jabbing each other. And we can do it just as quickly as we can throw a dart at a dartboard.

There's one more verse I'd like to share with you.

> The words of the reckless pierce like swords,
> but the tongue of the wise brings healing. (Prov. 12:18)

Taking those shots at each other? God calls it reckless. Saying hurtful things is like jabbing someone with a sword. But the second half of this verse talks about what it looks like to be wise. A wise person doesn't hurt with their tongue but uses words that bring help and hope, encouragement and healing.

What if we mark off forty days on the calendar and ask God to help us talk nicely to each other? So, for forty days, we'd make a real effort not to talk mean to each other. If we actually do that, I think we'll find that we like it so much, we won't want to stop when the forty days is up! What do you say . . . would you like to commit to doing that for forty days?

A Special Word for Parents

Mom and Dad, you'll set the tone in the family by how you talk to each other as well. Why not try the forty-day challenge yourselves?

Time to Burn

THEME: Laziness / time is a gift; we're not to waste it but use it wisely.

 ## THINGS YOU'LL NEED

- ☐ Safety glasses for each of the kids
- ☐ Plumber's propane torch, available at any hardware store. You know the type . . . with the small blue cylinder and the nice nozzle where the flame will come out. They're small and usually about $20—and so-o-o impressive when you light them. There's something about that blue flame that really gets kids' attention. If a torch is out of the question, you can do this devotional over a campfire or fire pit. You could even use a lighter, preferably a stick type.
- ☐ Flint spark torch igniter—if you're buying the plumber's torch, you'll need this as an easy, safe way to ignite it. Buy it at the hardware store with the propane torch; it's usually not more than $6 or $7.
- ☐ Bucket of water or a hose

☐ Items to burn. Get creative here. It could be food items (bread, hot-dogs, marshmallows). Burning a hole in a box of a favorite cereal is always fun. What about sports trading cards? Just be careful not to burn anything that may give off harmful smoke—or anything that is flammable itself. You'll also want to have some cash on hand. Don't worry, you won't burn it unless you want to, but either way it will make a great illustration. Put all your burn items in a bag.

Advance Prep

If you've never lit a plumber's torch before, you'll want to give that a try in advance. You'll like it. Maybe you're thinking of using a lighter instead because you won't use a plumber's torch after this devotional? Nonsense. A plumber's torch is a great way to light candles on a birthday cake! The kids will love it, and you'll never burn your fingers on those pesky matches again.

Next, find a safe place to burn your items. This isn't the type of devotional to do indoors—no matter how much you think you can control the fire. Let's not even go there, okay? Take this one outside. Do you have a patch of dirt somewhere in the yard? A kiddie sandbox? Either of those would make a great location choice. Make sure you have a running hose within reach too, or at least a bucket of water.

Running the Activity

Fire up the torch and announce that you're going to have some fun burning things. Pull something from the bag, place it on the ground, and torch it. Or maybe lay some of the things out and ask the kids what they'd like you to burn next. Keep the money out of sight for now.

The kids may have an idea of something to burn that you hadn't thought of. If they suggest something that sounds fun, go ahead and do that. Just don't take too long with the burn portion of this devotional. You don't want their attention to fade.

Now pull out the cash and ask them what they'd think about burning some of it. Likely you'll get some protests, but then again, they may encourage it. It's totally your call . . . but burning a dollar or two could be something that etches the point of this lesson into their minds even more.

Another way to really make this lesson stick is to let your kids do some of the burning. You're not teaching them to be pyromaniacs. All we're talking about here is letting them hold and aim the torch at something sitting on the ground. Explain to them that you're not playing with fire. You're using fire to teach an important life lesson. It's a lesson you want to burn into their brains . . . and in this case, there's no better way to do it than with fire.

Once you've had your burn time, turn off the gas to the propane torch. Remember, that nozzle will stay hot for a while. Then take the hose or bucket and thoroughly douse the burned items. Make sure there are no embers or sparks left. Nothing smoldering.

Teaching the Lesson

Now talk to the kids about how much fun it was to burn the items.

Did you have a favorite thing that I burned?

How would you like it if I went to your bedroom and brought out some of your special things to burn? Would that be a bad idea?

How did you feel when I burned (or almost burned) the cash?

It's one thing to burn worthless items like the marshmallows or bread or (*fill in the blank*). But to burn things that actually have value—like the money? That's just dumb, right? That is a total waste.

There's something else that we tend to burn or waste. All of us do. And it's extremely valuable. Anybody want to guess what it is? TIME.

- Time is a gift from God, just like a birthday gift. We only get so much time in a day . . . or in our lifetime.
- Time is more valuable than money. Just ask a billionaire dying of some deadly disease. He or she would trade in their billions if it would buy them a healthy body—and more time on earth.

Imagine taking all your birthday presents outside and making a bonfire out of them instead of opening and enjoying them. That would be crazy, wouldn't it?

But what are we doing with the gift of time that God has given us? Would he be happy with how we're using it? If we waste time . . . if we tend to be lazy and don't use our time productively, it's like we're torching a very valuable gift given to us by God.

Summing It Up

We all need a little downtime. But sometimes we can spend too much time on our devices. Too many hours spent staring at a screen—and not really using our time to do anything that will do some eternal good.

Sometimes there's work to be done. Let's not procrastinate; let's not waste that time. We want to get at our work when we have the chance to do it. If we do that, we'll be building good work habits. If we stall on the work we need to do, we'll learn to be lazy. Eventually, we'll be in the habit of being lazy, and it will catch up with us. Check out this verse from the Bible. A "sluggard" is simply a lazy person.

> Sluggards do not plow in season;
>> so at harvest time they look but find nothing. (Prov. 20:4)

The verse is saying that a lazy person doesn't get their work done when they should, when they have the chance. Later, they'll wish they had. They'll miss out in some way, like the farmer in the verse who had no food to eat.

Laziness doesn't give you an easier life. A lazy person finds that life actually gets harder and harder.

> The way of the sluggard is blocked with thorns,
>> but the path of the upright is a highway. (Prov. 15:19)

The Bible tells us that those who are upright—those who follow God and the principles he's given us to live by—travel on a highway by comparison. It's those who use their time wisely and aren't lazy who truly find life is smoother and has less bumps in the road.

Let's use the time God gives us for good things. Instead of being lazy, let's be careful not to waste the gift of time God gives us, okay?

> Be very careful, then, how you live—not as unwise but as wise, making the most of every opportunity, because the days are evil. (Eph. 5:15–16)

Parable of the Stock Car Race

THEME: Following God brings us on a journey, a life of purpose. Following the world is traveling in meaningless circles.

THINGS YOU'LL NEED

- ☐ A trip to a local stock car race. Google this, or ask around. If there is a track or speedway within two hours of you, it's totally worth the trip.
- ☐ If going to a stock car race is absolutely out of reach, consider finding some YouTube clips of races. You're not looking for recordings of longer races, but the shorter variety you'd find at local tracks.

Advance Prep

There's no other advance prep other than locating that stock car racetrack. Now, if you're thinking *Maybe I'll skip this one*, let me convince you otherwise. This lesson will convey an essential truth in a powerful way your kids will never forget. Don't shortcut this one. Your kids really, really need to hear this.

Ultimately, we're going to steer the conversation to a "big picture" application. Ask the kids to describe what they saw at the races—to boil it down to just a short statement. Take whatever they give you and work with it. When I did this with our boys, they responded with something like, "We saw a bunch of guys driving around in a circle trying to get ahead of each other." Then one of my other sons added "And they ended up right where they started . . . most of them with nothing."

That's basically where you'll want to steer this conversation. It will set you up perfectly to talk about life—and the way most people live it.

Running the Activity

When you get to the stock car race, just enjoy your time with the family. There will probably be a series of races. You may want each member of the family to choose their own individual car to cheer for with every new race.

After your time at the races is over, you'll teach the lesson in the car as you drive home. Or you may want to stop for food or snacks on your way back to talk it over with them. The nice thing about stopping is that it allows you to use your notes.

Teaching the Lesson

So, tell me about your favorite parts of the races.

The truth is many people live their lives like a stock car race.

- They're trying to get ahead of others. They may cut others off or even bump others to accomplish that. But in reality, they're only going in circles. They're not really going anywhere of true significance.
- They end up pretty much where they started . . . with nothing that counts in the long run. They are empty-handed when it comes to things that matter for eternity.

That's the way of the world. If you choose to follow the world's ways, you'd better get ready for the oval track. You won't be going anyplace that will matter for eternity.

But if you choose to go with God . . . if you dedicate yourself to trusting and following Jesus . . . he won't lead you around in circles. He'll take you on a real journey.

> Trust in the LORD with all your heart
> and lean not on your own understanding;
> in all your ways submit to him,
> and he will make your paths straight. (Prov. 3:5–6)

If we choose the journey God has planned for us, we may bump others—not to get ahead of them but to impact them for the Lord. God's path for us may seem boring at times, or exciting, or treacherous. But if we're traveling with him, it will be the best route, and one that will fill us with joy and purpose.

> You make known to me the path of life;
> you will fill me with joy in your presence,
> with eternal pleasures at your right hand. (Ps. 16:11)

Summing It Up

God has a plan for each of us. A life full of purpose.

> For we are God's handiwork, created in Christ Jesus to do good works, which God prepared in advance for us to do. (Eph. 2:10)

The devil and his demons would like to see us travel in meaningless circles. They'd like to see us crash. They'd like to take us out of the race, so we don't accomplish the things God has planned for us. We don't want that to happen, and it will be hard for the enemy to get near us if we stay close to God ourselves.

At that racetrack there were bleachers filled with fans cheering the drivers on. When we follow God's course for us, we have others cheering us on as well. Those who have taken God's journey mapped for them long ago. Those who have raced well.

> Therefore, since we are surrounded by such a great cloud of witnesses, let us throw off everything that hinders and the sin that so easily entangles. And let us run with perseverance the race marked out for us, fixing our eyes on Jesus, the pioneer and perfecter of faith. (Heb. 12:1–2)

Do you want God's course for your life? Tell him. And dedicate yourself to following him—even when that journey may get hard. Even if that means saying no to some things. At times, God's path may not appear to be the best, the most fun, or even the safest, but it is the only one that truly is all of those.

> The highway of the upright avoids evil;
>   those who guard their ways preserve their lives. (Prov. 16:17)

It's my prayer that you don't go the way most people do in this world, but steer your life so that you're always following Jesus on the journey he has planned for you.

Food Frenzy

THEME: God gives us time, resources, and the freedom to choose how we use them. We must choose wisely.

THINGS YOU'LL NEED

- ☐ A little cash for the kids to spend at the grocery store: $3–5 is generally enough. You could give this amount to each of the kids, or if you want to keep them together as a group, you may want to make it $5 or $10 total.
- ☐ A trip to the grocery store

Advance Prep

No advance prep needed, except to have the right denominations of cash on hand for the kids to spend at the grocery store. If you're going to give them each $3, it would be nice to give them three singles.

Running the Activity

Take the family to the grocery store. Depending on their ages, either you'll stay near the checkout and let them go through the store as a group, or you'll walk through the store with them. Either way, they'll make all buying decisions on their own—without any input from you.

Explain to them that you are giving them this money to buy anything to eat or drink that they want. If there is change left after their purchases, it all goes back to you. Also tell them they only have ten minutes to make their decisions and be back at the checkout.

After the kids have made their selections and paid for their purchases, go back to the house and have them spread out their goodies on the kitchen table. I imagine you'll see a lot of junk food. Chips. Candy. Soda. That's perfect. You're all set up to teach some important truth.

Teaching the Lesson

Make some general observations about what they've purchased, without sounding critical. Okay, I don't see any bread, fresh fruit, or vegetables. I'm seeing a lot of junk food here. Lots of things to snack on, but not much with any real nutritional value.

What might happen if you ate only junk food all the time? Do you imagine over the long run you'd get stronger, or do you think it may weaken you a bit? Might your body have a harder time fighting off germs?

You were given three things when you went to the grocery store:

- Time (ten minutes)
- Resources (in this case, some cash)
- Freedom (to choose how you'd spend your time and cash)

It looks like you chose to spend it mostly on snacks or junk food—things that make you weaker over the long run. And that's okay; it was just an activity we were doing.

But the important thing is that this shopping trip is like life in many ways. God gives us the same three things:

- He gives us time on earth . . . our lifetime. Twenty-four hours a day.
- He gives us resources. That could include money, sure, but think about the bigger things he gives us, like abilities, skills, strength, health, brains, opportunities, family, friends, and so on.
- He gives us the freedom to choose how we spend our time . . . and how we spend all the resources he gives us.

Too often, we take those three gifts from God—time, resources, and freedom—and spend them on things that have no "spiritual nutritional value." Can anybody guess what I mean by that?

Summing It Up

The Bible encourages us to think carefully . . . to be wise about how we spend the gifts of time, resources, and freedom that God gives us. We live in a dangerous, evil world—and the devil and his demons would like to destroy us and keep us distracted with things that won't build us spiritually at all.

Be very careful, then, how you live—not as unwise but as wise, making the most of every opportunity, because the days are evil. (Eph. 5:15–16)

Yes, God gives us freedom, but the Bible reminds us not to use this gift to just do whatever we feel like doing.

You, my brothers and sisters, were called to be free. But do not use your freedom to indulge the flesh; rather, serve one another humbly in love. (Gal. 5:13)

Even though we are free in so many ways, we still belong to God, don't we? He created us. Died for us. Paid the price for our sins—and effectively bought us with his blood.

Live as free people, but do not use your freedom as a cover-up for evil; live as God's slaves. (1 Pet. 2:16)

God gives each of us the same three things. Let's remember to spend our time, resources, and freedom on things that will be good for us spiritually in the long run, things that will count for eternity. Let's "buy" things that will make us spiritually stronger, not weaker.

Good Goalie

THEME: Being diligent to keep sin out of our lives . . . instead of letting "little sins" slip by.

THINGS YOU'LL NEED

☐ Ideally, take the kids to a hockey or soccer game. It doesn't have to be a pro game, although if the kids are older, that would make it that much more special. As an option, you could just take the kids outside and play soccer or hockey with them. But realize the more effort you put into this—the more of an event you make it—the bigger the impact. This is especially true as the kids hit middle school and high school.

Advance Prep

None needed, unless you need to buy tickets to a game.

Running the Activity

For the sake of simplicity, I'm going to coach you through the rest of this lesson as if you're going to a hockey game. Just adapt things as needed if you choose a soccer game, or if you organize a game with the kids at home instead.

Take the kids to the game and just enjoy the time. Include snacks or soft drinks just to make the time more special and memorable. Do your best to make any activity you do for family devotions like this a really good experience for the kids. You can talk about the "lesson" of this devotional on the drive home—or better yet, stop someplace for a snack or pizza before you get back to the house.

Teaching the Lesson

Okay, who can tell me what the whole objective of a hockey (or soccer) game is? The team with the highest score wins, so it seems there are two main objectives:

1. Keep the opposition from scoring goals.
2. Ultimately, make at least one more goal than the opposing team.

Every player is essential, but with the first objective of the game in mind, who is one person the team probably couldn't survive without?

What did you notice about the goalie? Did they have more equipment or different equipment than the other players? With hockey, certainly the goalie wears some extra gear for protection. Players are going to be firing the puck at the goal—and sometimes the goalie is going to use their body to block it.

Did you notice how focused the goalie was every time the opposing team took a shot on the goal?

Can you imagine a goalie who felt it was okay to let a goal slide by now and then? No good goalie would do that, right? That one goal they let slide into the net could be the one that determines who wins the game.

Can you imagine a goalie who didn't bother to wear the protective gear for the game? Can you imagine a goalie guarding the goal without bothering to use their hockey stick?

That's sort of like us as Christians. We're like goalies. We've got opposition, the devil and his demons, taking shots at us. They're hoping to get us to mess up. Hoping they'll catch us off guard. Hoping we haven't geared up or prepared for their attack. Hoping we'll get sloppy and let some sin get past us and into our lives. Those sins can add up—and be a real game changer.

> How can a young person stay on the path of purity?
>> By living according to your word.
> I seek you with all my heart;
>> do not let me stray from your commands.
> I have hidden your word in my heart
>> that I might not sin against you. (Ps. 119:9–11)

The Bible encourages us to be strong—and to suit up for the game.

Finally, be strong in the Lord and in his mighty power. Put on the full armor of God, so that you can take your stand against the devil's schemes. For our struggle is not against flesh and blood, but against the rulers, against the authorities, against the powers of this dark world and against the spiritual forces of evil in the heavenly realms. Therefore put on the full armor of God, so that when the day of evil comes, you may be able to stand your ground, and after you have done everything, to stand. Stand firm then, with the belt of truth buckled around your waist, with the breastplate of righteousness in place, and with your feet fitted with the readiness that comes from the gospel of peace. In addition to all this, take up the shield of faith, with which you can extinguish all the flaming arrows of the evil one. Take the helmet of salvation and the sword of the Spirit, which is the word of God. (Eph. 6:10–17)

Summing It Up

Good goalies stay where they're supposed to be. They don't wander far from the net, leaving it unprotected. Sometimes we need to be careful that we are where we should be as Christians . . . not some-place we don't belong. That's one of the things that got King David in such trouble, isn't it? He was supposed to be in the game—on the battlefield (2 Sam. 11:1), as kings were expected to do.

But this time, David wasn't where he belonged. He wasn't out on the battlefield. He was wandering around on the roof, killing time. He was letting his eyes scroll to places they didn't belong. David didn't gear up for battle at all. He wasn't on guard. It might have seemed like a little thing at the time. The real battle was far away. He didn't sense he was about to get attacked. Ambushed. There didn't seem to be any real danger where David was.

But the enemy was ready. The enemy took a shot at David and tempted him with a woman who wasn't his wife. And instead of blocking that sin, he let it glide right into his life. The enemy scored a major, major goal on David that absolutely changed his life.

That tragic story makes for a good reminder. David, who was normally so good about keeping sin out of his life, let some slip by. It was something he grew to regret massively. Take a look at Psalm 51, which he wrote while he grieved over his huge mistake.

Kids, we must stay on guard. We need to keep ourselves where we need to be as Christians—and not wander off, leaving our "net" wide open. We need to protect our hearts and minds and remain alert against allowing sin inside.

Be on your guard; stand firm in the faith; be courageous; be strong. Do everything in love. (1 Cor. 16:13–14)

There are some places we just don't belong as followers of Christ. It may be places online. Sometimes even social media sites or exchanges just aren't appropriate. It may be with some friends—or in places they want us to go that just don't fit with being a disciple of Christ. If we give in to these temptations, we're exposing ourselves to trouble and leaving our goal unprotected, in a way. Sometimes we've got to stay in the net a bit more, guarding ourselves so that we keep sin from sliding into our lives. God can help us with that if we ask him, yes?

The Things We Carry

THEME: Jesus cares for us and shows it by offering to carry our worry, anxiety, and fear so we don't have to.

THINGS YOU'LL NEED

☐ Wheelbarrow. If you don't have one, likely you'll find a friend or neighbor who has one you can borrow. You could also swap out the wheelbarrow for a wagon, or do this at a grocery store parking lot and borrow one of their carts for the activity.

☐ Weight. An easy solution is construction sand that you'll find in the hardware store. You can get 60 lb. tubes for under $10. I'd pick up three of them, unless your kids are really young and can't handle that much weight. To drive home the point of this devotional, you want the weighted wheelbarrow, wagon, or cart to be a bit difficult to move with any real speed. If sandbags aren't an option, you can always use some of the kids as weight.

Advance Prep

You'll have the kids pushing a wheelbarrow or cart, or pulling a wagon, in a race against the clock. So you'll want to pick a place where you can do that. If you're using the shopping cart option, find a store with a huge parking lot so you can do this way out on the far edge of the lot where there shouldn't be any traffic or even any parked cars.

Running the Activity

Take the kids to the location you've chosen for the little race. Go over the course so they know exactly where to start and finish. Basically, you'll want them to race with the wheelbarrow or cart to a particular point and back. Explain that you'll be timing them—and go over some safety rules if this is in a parking lot.

The first time you do this, don't put any weight in that cart or wheelbarrow. Have one of your kids run the route while any other kids present cheer them on. Be sure to time them.

Once they've run that course with the unweighted cart, have them help you add the weight. Then have them run the course again. The time should be longer—and/or more tiring—especially if you built some turns into the course.

Okay, great job. Pack things up (and put the cart back in the corral, if applicable) and take the kids someplace where you can go over the lesson.

Teaching the Lesson

Obviously, it was a lot easier and quicker to run without the weight in that wheelbarrow. Can you imagine how hard it would be if the course were miles long? What if you had to push a wheelbarrow like this every day—all day—filled with weight like this? That would get old *fast*.

In life, sometimes we do a similar thing when we hold on to worry, anxiety, and fear. They're like weights slowing us down. They're always there, making everything we do more difficult.

There are many different types of weight we can carry with us. Jesus knows what it's like to carry the weight of the world on his shoulders.

- He was slandered by the Pharisees. They tried to destroy his reputation—claiming he did his miracles with the power of Satan instead of the power of God. These people were constantly trying to trip him up and twist his words. They hated him.
- People constantly misunderstood Jesus and accused him of wrong motives.
- Jesus grieved for the people who followed leaders who were blind themselves. That was a weight he carried, for sure.
- He had the devil test him over and over, trying to get him to mess up. And if he did mess up, that would have been the end of God's plan to save the world through Jesus.
- Jesus was betrayed by a disciple—and abandoned by his closest friends.

Yeah, Jesus knew quite a bit about carrying burdens, didn't he?

And there are weights—burdens—that we all tend to pick up. All kinds of fear. Many different cares and worries. And definitely various levels of anxiety. God never meant for us to carry these alone. He wants us to toss them his way . . . because he cares for us *that* much.

> When I am afraid, I put my trust in you.
>   In God, whose word I praise—
> in God I trust and am not afraid.
>   What can mere mortals do to me? (Ps. 56:3–4)

Sometimes trusting God is hard. But we work on that, reminding ourselves through past experiences and verses in the Bible that we can trust God—even with our fears. He is God . . . not a man. He is unlimited.

> Cast your cares on the LORD
> and he will sustain you;
> he will never let
> the righteous be shaken. (Ps. 55:22)

There are so many things that we really care about. Our cares can consume us with worry. But God cares for us so much that he wants to do the heavy lifting. I love that he will never let the righteous be shaken. Sometimes our whole world feels like it is shaking, doesn't it?

> Cast all your anxiety on him because he cares for you. (1 Pet. 5:7)

We weren't designed to carry all these problems and fears and concerns of life on our own. We have a Savior who cares. A rescuer. And that rescuer is Jesus. Right there in 1 Peter 5:7, he tells us that we must throw our burdens on him. Our problems *matter* to him. He cares about us and the loads we are carrying. Isn't that amazing?

Summing It Up

It is so easy to worry or to be anxious or to be fearful. The truth is, we live in a scary world filled with sin and evil and problems. Often there is good reason to be worried, fearful, or anxious. Living with such thoughts will slow us down in life, but it can be really hard to shed them. It's not quite as easy as dragging that weight out of the wheelbarrow (or cart) like we did after our race.

But God gives us some clues as to how to shed these things. Remember God is near each of us. That gives comfort and eases some fear right there. And we need to bring our cares and worries to him, knowing that he hears us. Unload on him. Also, sometimes we need to work at thinking about the good things . . . not dwelling on the worries.

The Lord is near. Do not be anxious about anything, but in every situation, by prayer and petition, with thanksgiving, present your requests to God. And the peace of God, which transcends all understanding, will guard your hearts and your minds in Christ Jesus.

Finally, brothers and sisters, whatever is true, whatever is noble, whatever is right, whatever is pure, whatever is lovely, whatever is admirable—if anything is excellent or praiseworthy—think about such things. Whatever you have learned or received or heard from me, or seen in me—put it into practice. And the God of peace will be with you. (Phil. 4:5–9)

That peace we experience may only last for a few moments. But then we repeat the procedure. As soon as the weight comes back on, we work at tossing it back to God again. Eventually our trust in him will grow stronger and stronger until we shed those anxious weights of fear and worry for good.

Read the book of Psalms. You'll see how often the psalmists were in a position of carrying some great fear or worry or anxious weight. It took all kinds of forms. Feeling down on themselves . . . feeling a world of opposition against them that was just too big and strong for them to handle. Fearing they weren't adequate. Feeling alone, unheard, and unseen. Feeling friends had betrayed them. Feeling others wanted to trip them up or see them fail. So many of the psalms show that the writer was feeling anxious, afraid, or weighted down with worry. As you read, you'll see how they turn the focus onto God and find comfort there.

A Special Word for Parents

Parents, anxiety is HUGE among youth today, even in Christian homes. Too many kids don't know how to shed this weight. Many don't even think it's possible. You need to help them in this area. And by the way, how are you doing with worry, fear, and anxiety? You need to work at this and find measures of victory . . . so you can help your kids.

Keep an eye on your kids. Ask them questions, choosing a good time and place to do it. Watch their eyes. Their body language. Research the telltale signs of dangerous anxiety and get them help if you suspect they need it. Sometimes our kids can be in a place that requires a professional counselor. That's nothing to be ashamed of. Our enemy is good at piling burdens on us and our kids. Sometimes the best help you can give them is to find a solid Christian counselor. One who can assist them with untangling the anxiety that has a chokehold on them.

So do that . . . find that Christian counselor. Ask around. Check with your pastor. Call an organization like Focus on the Family. They'll help you with those next steps. Just don't wait on this, okay? If your kid is carrying a burden of anxiety or worry or fear, they're likely exhausted from doing that. God wants them to learn to shed those—right onto him. With God's leading, you can help them unload the weight they're carrying . . . and teach them to place it all on Jesus.

One last thought. If you have a child struggling with worry, anxiety, or fear, it likely won't be solved with one lesson. You'll want to come back to this theme over and over. Check the table of contents for the devotionals Where Am I? and Smashed Tomatoes right here in this book.

Sometimes anxiety weighs us down because of sin we still feel guilty about—even though we've been forgiven. If that is a contributor to some of the anxiety any of your kids are feeling, check out the very next devotional in this book, The Depths of Love.

Also, take a look in the table of contents of both volume 1 and volume 2 of The Very Best, Hands-On, Kinda Dangerous Family Devotions for other lessons related to this topic of worry, fear, and anxiety.

If you're carrying anxious thoughts, fear, or worry, I get it. It's hard not to be burdened by those things. But Jesus tells us we're not to carry them. Sometimes we can't seem to figure out how to toss our load to Jesus, even if we want to. So, talk to me about that, okay? Our God really can help . . . and I want to help you experience the freedom and peace we can have in Jesus as we shed the weight of our worries, anxiety, and fears by tossing them to him.

The Depths of Love

THEME: When God forgives, that sin is gone for good.

THINGS YOU'LL NEED

- ☐ Light-colored, smooth-surfaced rocks—a half-dozen or so for each of the kids. You want something big enough to write on with a marker but small enough to fit in the palm of your hand. (A ten-pound bag of baking potatoes can make a good substitute for the rocks. They sink—which is what you want—but if you're on a beach with heavy surf, they could wash ashore if you don't throw them far enough. That would defeat the purpose of the devotional a bit.)
- ☐ Fine-point permanent markers (one for each of the kids)
- ☐ Body of water, such as a river, lake, or ocean
- ☐ United States Coast Guard–approved life jackets for the kids, if appropriate. If you do this from a dock or pier, definitely wear life jackets.

Advance Prep

Gather the rocks or potatoes and do a test with the marker, making sure it writes clearly on the surface. You'll be throwing these out into a body of water with the kids. Find a good place that is remote enough where you won't risk hitting swimmers, boats, piers—or anything else.

Running the Activity

Take the kids to that body of water, and pile up the rocks (or potatoes) on shore. Life jackets are always encouraged when you're around water, unless you believe your kids are old enough and solid swimmers.

Announce that you'd like them to take a marker and a rock and write down a sin they can think of that God has forgiven them for. Lying. Pride. Selfishness. Unforgiveness. It can be general or specific. This isn't anything they're going to show to you or to anyone else. Once they write a sin on a rock, have them hurl it out as far from shore as they can. Now, you'll want to participate as well. It's a good thing for kids to see that Mom and Dad are aware of their own sin.

Repeat this exercise of writing sins and hurling them out into the water until all the rocks are gone. Then you're ready to transition to the lesson and the nugget of truth.

Teaching the Lesson

The rocks we threw out into the water are gone. Who is going to go looking for them? Anyone? No. Nobody in their right mind would strap on a scuba tank and search the depths just to find those rocks. They're gone for good.

And that is the way it is with the sins we've committed. When Jesus forgives us, those sins are gone forever. The Bible gives us a number of pictures of what forgiveness is like. In the verse below, God compares that complete forgiveness to hurling our sins into the depths of the sea.

> You will again have compassion on us;
>   you will tread our sins underfoot
>   and hurl all our iniquities into the depths of the sea.
>   (Mic. 7:19)

What a great picture! Our sins—gone. Buried at the bottom of the sea, never to be seen again. And this is why we serve him with gratitude . . . for what he has done for us. Our sins condemn us, and when we ask Jesus to forgive us, it's as if he takes all the wrong things we've said or thought or done and hurls them into the deepest part of the sea. A place that nobody will go looking for it, including him.

If God has forgiven our sins and won't bring them back up to the surface again, how should we forgive others when they sin against us?

Since God has forgiven our sins—all those wrong things we thought and said and did that held us prisoner and condemned us to hell—how should we show gratitude to him for what he has done for us?

Summing It Up

When God forgives, the Bible says he "remembers our sin no more."

> I, even I, am he who blots out
>   your transgressions, for my own sake,
>   and remembers your sins no more. (Isa. 43:25)

In another passage, God states he has removed that sin as far away from us as "the east is from the west." Those two never touch each other.

> For as high as the heavens are above the earth,
>   so great is his love for those who fear him;
> as far as the east is from the west,
>   so far has he removed our transgressions from us.
>   (Ps. 103:11–12)

If God chooses to remember our sins no more, and if God has removed our sins so far from us that they will never touch us again, then we should let go of them too. Sometimes even though we are forgiven by God, we choose to remember our own sins. When we do that, we essentially let our enemy, the devil, beat us up. Constant reminders of our sins can make us fearful, anxious, and definitely discouraged. Remembering our sins can make us think we are so unworthy of God that we shy away from him, or from serving him. Remember, every one of us is unworthy of God's love and forgiveness . . . which is one more reason to love our God all the more, isn't it?

When God forgives, that sin is gone for good. Instead of remembering our sins, let's remember how much he forgave us and show him more appreciation for all he has done for us!

Essential Anchors

THEME: We need anchors in our lives to keep us from drifting away from where God wants us to be.

 ## THINGS YOU'LL NEED

☐ Access to a boat with an anchor and a nice, long anchor line. Rentals can be expensive. Ask around at church or at work. Many boat owners would love to give your family a short ride. And remember, you don't need anything fancy. A fishing boat or a rowboat will do. It just has to be big enough to fit your family on board.

☐ Coast Guard–approved life jackets for all who will be in the boat

☐ Homemade anchor. This is in addition to the anchor already in the boat. Basically, you'll use a plastic bag intended for leaves or garbage. A heavy-duty (3 mil thick) bag is sturdy enough to do the job. Add some kind of drink your kids will love as a surprise treat for while you're on the boat. Soda? Gatorade? Anything works. Put it in the bag and pack ice around it. Add a couple of heavy rocks so the bag will sink like an anchor.

☐ Zip tie to close the top of the bag

☐ Rope to use for an anchor line. Longer is better. Even if the water is generally shallow, a 50–100' rope is recommended. The longer the line, the more effective your anchor will be. An 8 lb. anchor can hold a 3,000 lb. boat in place if your line is long enough.

Advance Prep

You'll want to test your homemade anchor in advance. When I threw my makeshift anchor overboard for the first time, the thing didn't sink, even with the rocks. There was too much air trapped in the bag—and, of course, ice floats. So check this out ahead of time using a barrel or tank full of water or a pool, lake, or whatever. It's important that the anchor actually sinks.

If you have the same problem getting your anchor to sink as I did at first, add more weight to the bag and squeeze out more air. I simply poked some holes into the black plastic bag, and it sank just fine.

Running the Activity

When you're actually out in the boat with the kids, find a good place to stop. Cut the motor or stop rowing. Tell the kids that the objective is to keep the boat in exactly the spot where it is now—and that's the job of the anchor.

Now have one of the kids toss both the real and the homemade anchors overboard. Remember, use plenty of anchor line. Even if the water is only a few feet deep, using more line will help the anchors hold the boat in place better. Ask them these two questions:

> If we didn't use an anchor, is it possible that we'd drift from this spot, even if we don't notice any wind or waves?
>
> If we didn't set an anchor, what kinds of things might happen to us—and the boat eventually—if we *did* float away and also didn't stop our craft from drifting?

You're all prepared to teach the lesson. Well done.

Teaching the Lesson

Every boat needs an anchor. It gets a grip on the bottom and keeps us from drifting into trouble. It's the same with our Christian life. We need "anchors," things that help keep us from drifting away from God—and into trouble and danger. What kinds of things can be good anchors in our lives? I'm not talking about things that hold us back from getting in trouble. I'm referring to things that keep us from drifting from God—and the principles he's given us to live by.

- Love: the love we have for God and for our Lord Jesus.
- Our salvation: knowing our sin has been forgiven should fill us with gratitude that anchors us to the Lord. "We have this hope as an anchor for the soul, firm and secure" (Heb. 6:19).
- Prayer: asking God to keep us true to him and increase our faith.
- The Bible: regularly reading God's Word reminds us of the truth . . . and the things we should hold to firmly.
- Parents, grandparents, family: when we're open with each other, we can help encourage each other in ways that keep us all from drifting.

- Church: part of the reason we go to church is to be with other believers. All of us can help and encourage each other not to drift.
- Friends: good friends should be encouraging us to do the good and right things. If they encourage us to do things that are bad, we need new anchors.
- Our conviction: the boundaries we set up, our morals, our code of ethics, a good reputation that we want to build—all of these can work as good and essential anchors to fight drift.

If the anchor wasn't connected to the boat when we threw it overboard, it wouldn't keep the boat from drifting. And it's the same with each of these things we've just mentioned. We need a real connection to God. We need to truly be in the Word. We need to attend church regularly and consistently. We need to stay connected to our families and be open and honest with them, especially our parents. In all these ways, if our personal connection is weak, it won't serve as a very effective anchor.

In other words, we can't just go through the motions. We need to hold on to these anchors tight.

By this gospel you are saved, if you hold firmly to the word I preached to you. Otherwise, you have believed in vain. (1 Cor. 15:2)

Let us hold unswervingly to the hope we profess, for he who promised is faithful. (Heb. 10:23)

Timothy, my son, I am giving you this command in keeping with the prophecies once made about you, so that by recalling them you may fight the battle well, holding on to faith and a good conscience, which some have rejected and so have suffered shipwreck with regard to the faith. (1 Tim. 1:18–19)

I love the way this passage in 1 Timothy uses the word *shipwreck*. That is exactly the point. If we don't have anchors that keep us from drifting, we'll end up in some kind of a shipwreck ourselves.

Summing It Up

Ultimately, as we hold tight to the Lord, we find that he's also holding us as well. That's a firm anchor!

> I cling to you;
>> your right hand upholds me. (Ps. 63:8)

Now it's time to pull up your homemade anchor. Open the plastic bag, and there will be nice, cold soda—or whatever else you put inside to drink. Use that as one last little reminder.

Sometimes we think of anchors as holding us back. But anchors do more than that. Having the right anchors in our life will keep us from drifting into sin and danger. And having the right anchors generally has a way of bringing us great rewards.

How Can a Good God Allow This?

How can a good God allow bad things to happen to "good" people?

THINGS YOU'LL NEED

☐ Glow sticks, the type you find in the dollar store. Pick up one for you and one for each of the kids who will be in the lesson time. A variety of shapes, sizes, and colors is ideal.

Advance Prep

No advance prep needed other than to review the lesson—which is an extremely important one. The theme poses a question that your kids will wrestle with at some point. More Christians have become disillusioned with God—or have drifted from the faith—because they didn't have a solid, balanced answer. How *can* a good God allow bad things to happen? Your kids need you to help them process this, and you'll do exactly that with this devotional.

Running the Activity

Gather the kids in a room that can go dark with the flip of a switch—and bring the glow sticks with you.

Pull out your glow stick, tear off the packaging, and explain how the thing works. Show them the plastic tube, explaining it is filled with a chemical. Suspended in that chemical is a small glass vial containing a second chemical. In order to get the stick to glow, you bend it until you break that glass vial. (*Don't actually do that yet . . . just talk it through for now.*) Then you shake it up so that the two solutions create a glowing chemical reaction.

Once you explain how the glow stick works, move on to sharing the truth of this lesson.

Teaching the Lesson

How can a good God allow bad things to happen to Christians, innocent kids, or any other good, decent people? Have you ever wondered about that? It's an important question, and one we'll answer today.

I can think of three basic reasons God allows bad things to happen to good people.

First, we live in a sinful world, so it's natural that bad things happen. People get sick. People die. People make bad choices that hurt others. A computer virus attacks all computers, regardless of how nice the people are that own them. That's a picture of what happened when sin entered this world. Sin impacts everyone . . . good people and bad people. But still, how can God just sit there and let it happen? Why doesn't he *do* something?

Actually, he did. He sent his Son to pay the price for our sins. For all of us who have received that gift, he promises that he'll never leave us. He'll walk with us through all the good and bad things in life. And because of Jesus's death and resurrection, he's already rescued us from the ultimate penalty of sin. So, God already put the solution in motion. Someday, when he makes all things new, bad things won't happen anymore. But until then, sin will still hurt the good and the bad.

Second, sometimes he allows bad things to happen to wake people up. Sometimes a parent who is out shopping has trouble keeping their little kids close. When Junior wanders off, sometimes Mom or Dad might hide, watching the child the whole time. There is a moment when Junior panics, realizing they're lost. That might seem like a cruel thing for the parent to do, but it is about teaching the child to stay close, so they don't get seriously lost or hurt someday. Sometimes God allows bad things to happen to us so that we pay attention and work to stay closer to God . . . for our own good.

To help explain the third reason bad things happen to good people, I'd like each of you take a glow stick. Don't unwrap it yet. In a minute I'll turn out the lights—and you can bend your glow stick until you break it, and we'll enjoy the glow as we talk about the third reason God allows bad things to happen to good people, even to Christians.

Christians can be a lot like a glow stick in its packaging. We might look fine and polished. Perfect. But a glow stick on display in its packaging is not doing what it was made to do. As a first step, we have to strip away that wrapper, don't we?

Sometimes we aren't doing what God made *us* to do. Sometimes we aren't becoming the person God intended us to be. So, God strips away some things from our lives. (*Peel off the glow stick wrapper.*)

And he bends us in some kind of hard situation until he breaks us. (*Bend the glow stick until the glass vial inside breaks.*)

He shakes up our entire world. (*Shake the glow stick so that the chemicals mix well, and the entire stick starts glowing.*) And it is then that a change happens *inside* us. Our hearts change. And **Christ shines through us like he never could before.** That is the third reason.

> You are the light of the world. A town built on a hill cannot be hidden. Neither do people light a lamp and put it under a bowl. Instead, they put it on its stand, and it gives light to everyone in the house. In the same way, let your light shine before others, that they may see your good deeds and glorify your Father in heaven. (Matt. 5:14–16)

Summing It Up

When we experience hard things in life, or go through tough experiences that seem to be bending and breaking us, it often makes us cling tighter to the Lord. We see our need for him. We draw closer. Stay closer.

When we go through those times that seem to shake up our entire world, our perspective changes. We tend to seek him more, and as we do, our love for him increases. When our love for the Lord grows even in the hard times, people see Jesus in us.

As God shows his faithfulness to us through hard times, we get stronger than ever. We mature as Christians. We are better able to handle life in a tough, sinful world. And as we do so, we can be a great example to others. We can help others through their hard times too.

> Praise be to the God and Father of our Lord Jesus Christ, the Father of compassion and the God of all comfort, who comforts us in all our troubles, so that we can comfort those in any trouble with the comfort we ourselves receive from God. For just as we share abundantly

in the sufferings of Christ, so also our comfort abounds through Christ. (2 Cor. 1:3–5)

Tragically, some Christians distance themselves from God when bad things happen. Instead of drawing closer to the Lord . . . instead of letting Jesus shine through them when they feel broken . . . they become angry or bitter or confused. Don't let that happen to you—because now you know the answer to that very difficult question: How can our good, loving God allow bad things to happen to good people, even Christians?

1. We live in a sinful world, so bad things happen to everyone, reminding all people that they need a Savior.
2. Bad things tend to make us follow the Lord more closely, which is definitely for our good.
3. Hard, crushing things can change us on the inside so God shines through us, and we become the people he designed us to be.

Remember, no matter what reason God allows the bad things, it all works out for our good in the long run. We have his word on that!

And we know that in all things God works for the good of those who love him, who have been called according to his purpose. (Rom. 8:28)

Fishing Lesson

THEME: Resisting temptation.

═══ **THINGS YOU'LL NEED** ═══

☐ A fishing trip, a visit to a sporting goods store that sells fishing lures, or a chance to look through a fisher's tackle box. You can make any one of these options work.

☐ Fishing lures. Buy a lure for each of the kids. You can get ones that look like a fish for $3–4 each on sale. By giving each of them a lure, you'll leave them with a great reminder that they have an enemy who is fishing for them. You can remove the hooks with a set of pliers, if you'd like, and a lure makes a great key fob or zipper pull.

Advance Prep

No real advance prep other than to decide how you'll show them the lures (going fishing / visiting a store / viewing a tackle box) and picking up a lure for each of the kids who will be present during the lesson time.

Running the Activity

Whether you take the kids fishing, look through a tackle box, or stroll down the aisle in a sporting goods store, you'll end up in the same place: looking at lures. While looking at all the lures, here are four questions to ask the kids.

1. Why do fishers have so many lures? (Different lures are for different fish.)
2. How can fish be fooled by some of these lures—especially ones with big hooks hanging off them? (Maybe the water is murky, or it looks like real food to the fish. Maybe the lure goes by so quickly that fish are fooled, or maybe the fish see the hooks but think they can avoid them.)
3. What kinds of things do fishers do with the fish they catch? (Throw them back, use them for bait, eat them, or mount them as a trophy.)
4. What is one character trait fishers generally have—at least while they're fishing? (Patience.)

Now you're all set up to move into the lesson. If you're at a store, you may want to relocate. If you have a tackle box, it would be nice to have that with you as you teach.

Teaching the Lesson

Did you know that the devil and his demons are fishers? They have lots of lures. They know what we like—what we're hungry for. And they're patient. They'll cast things by us over and over and over, hoping that one time we'll take a bite. Hoping we're hungry enough for whatever that lure is. Hoping the waters of right and wrong are murky enough for us to take the bait. Hoping we'll talk ourselves into believing that somehow we can avoid the hooks and not get caught and reeled in.

What are some lures the devil and his demons might cast by friends of yours, or kids your age? When somebody takes the bait, what kinds of things do you think the devil and his demons might do with those they catch?

- Do they sometimes mount them as a trophy for everyone to see, making sure the word gets out? *Hey, look at what this Christian got caught doing!*
- Do they toss them back, releasing them from the hooks without any bad consequences? Not likely.
- Do they devour them sometimes?

  > Be alert and of sober mind. Your enemy the devil prowls around like a roaring lion looking for someone to devour. Resist him, standing firm in the faith. (1 Pet. 5:8–9)

- How might the devil and his demons use somebody as bait? Could it be that someone who gives in to temptation doesn't get "reeled in" right away? They may wait a while on that. The person who failed to resist temptation is still on the hook, but the enemy fisher lets the line run free for a bit. It might actually look like the person beat the hooks—and that giving in to that temptation resulted in no negative consequences for them at all. Do you see how easily the enemy can use them as bait that way?

Summing It Up

> For your ways are in full view of the LORD,
>   and he examines all your paths.
> The evil deeds of the wicked ensnare them;
>   the cords of their sins hold them fast.
> For lack of discipline they will die,
>   led astray by their own great folly. (Prov. 5:21–23)

These verses talk about someone who gave in to temptation. They are "held fast"—or held tight—by the cords of their sins, like a fish being reeled in with a hook in its mouth.

If we give in to temptation and sin, we need to confess that to God. He is the one who can free us, right? That's why God sent Jesus: to free us from our sin—and the penalty for sin.

A fish who thinks a lure is lunch soon becomes lunch. Sometimes we can think of the Bible as a book of dos and don'ts. But it's a whole lot more than that. It's a survival guide. We have an enemy who is fishing for us, and the Bible tells us how to avoid getting caught by the devil's lures.

I have a lure for each of you. You can stick it in a drawer, or if you want, we can take the hooks off with a pair of pliers so you can use it as a zipper pull or key fob. But whenever you see it, remember you have an enemy fishing for you. Let it remind you to be on your guard and to ask God to help you resist that temptation!

> Submit yourselves, then, to God. Resist the devil, and he will flee from you. (James 4:7)

Nobody Will Know

THEME: God sees everything . . . so we never really get away with doing wrong things.

THINGS YOU'LL NEED

☐ Plenty of toilet paper . . . enough to TP somebody's house

☐ An accomplice at that person's home who can video the prank without your kids knowing

Advance Prep

The big thing here is working out someone's home to TP. It should be a friend or family member, for sure. You'll want to pick a home that has a yard with enough light—even at night—so that someone in the home can take video that will be clear enough to capture the deed on film. Testing this ahead of time is a really good idea.

Work out all the details with your accomplice. What time you'll arrive at their house. How the house will need to look empty . . . like nobody is home. And, most importantly, where you'll need to position the kids so your accomplice inside the home can get a clear video of them pranking the house.

Running the Activity

Tell the kids that you're going to TP the house of whichever relative/family friend you've selected. Explain that the objective, of course, is not to get caught in the process. So you'll work together as a family to pull off the perfect prank!

When you get to their house, they'll want to have all their inside lights off, so it appears nobody is home. They may also want to park their car a block or so away, adding to the illusion.

Now lead the kids in a quick and quiet mission of toilet papering that home. Be sure to get them all gathered in the right spot where they'll be clearly caught on video. Once you're done, don't hang around. Hop in the car and go home—or someplace where you can teach the lesson.

As soon as you leave, your accomplice can start texting you video clips they caught of the family. Maybe they can send a message that says something like, "I think you'll find the attached video very interesting." That's perfect. You're all set up to teach the lesson.

Teaching the Lesson

For a few moments you might talk about how all of you got away with the prank. Nobody caught you, and you made a clean getaway.

By this time the texts should have stacked up on your phone. Open the texts—and show the kids the videos that catch them in the act of pranking the house. Now you're ready to transition into the spiritual truth you want to teach with this lesson.

So, even though it totally looked like we got away with this, it's clear we were wrong.

It was fun doing this when we thought we weren't going to get caught, and we figured nobody would find out what we did. But if we'd known they were watching us the whole time, would we have still pranked their house? Probably not.

Life is like this sometimes. We sometimes do things we probably wouldn't do if we knew we'd be caught. But the truth? We *always* get caught—because God sees everything we do. Listen to these Bible verses.

> For your ways are in full view of the LORD,
>   and he examines all your paths. (Prov. 5:21)

> For God will bring every deed into judgment,
>   including every hidden thing,
>   whether it is good or evil. (Eccl. 12:14)

Summing It Up

Now, since it's clear you were caught, you'll want to pile the family back into the car—and go back to the scene of the crime. Together, you'll have to clean up the mess, right? You might want to let the kids know that you set up this whole thing with your accomplice for the purpose of teaching an important lesson in a way they wouldn't likely forget. It would be nice if your accomplice came outside and joked around with the family, letting them know that all is forgiven.

When the toilet paper is completely cleaned up, you might make one last point.

When we mess up—and are forgiven—usually we'll still need to help clean up our mess. That's called *restitution*, and you did a good job. But, of course, what is the best thing? To do what's right—even when we think nobody will know if we choose to do something wrong. If there's something we're tempted to do that might require restitution if we get caught, the wise choice is not to do it in the first place! We need to realize that God sees everything . . . so we will always get caught.

This Little Light of Mine

THEME: We're to be an example to our friends—and to the world—of what Jesus is like.

 ═══ **THINGS YOU'LL NEED** ═══

- ☐ Fuel-burning camping lantern. If you don't have one, ask around at work or church. Likely someone will have one you can borrow. (A large flashlight or battery-powered lantern can work as a replacement, though it is not ideal.)
- ☐ Small pocket flashlight
- ☐ Matches and fuel (if using a camping lantern)

Optional: often you can purchase a keychain with a miniature lantern on it that actually works. I've seen them in four-packs for $8 online. Pick one up for each of the kids—and for yourself too. If you're going the flashlight route, you may want to purchase a keychain flashlight for yourself and each of the kids. Either way, mini-lantern or mini-flashlight, by having one for each of the kids, you'll multiply the power of this devotional. The kids will be reminded of the lesson every time they see their keychain.

Advance Prep

Pick up the lantern or flashlight, and buy the keychains if you decide to do that option. Also, when you get to the teaching part of this lesson, you'll want to be someplace dark. If you're using a lantern, you'll want to be outside for proper ventilation.

Unless you've got a really, really dark place outside, you may want to sum up the lesson indoors. That's where you'll need the small flashlight mentioned in the Things You'll Need list.

Be sure to select a room that will be totally dark when the lights are turned off. A basement or bathroom without windows works fine. If you don't have a windowless space, consider taping a large black garbage bag over the window so you can get the room really dark.

Running the Activity

Light the lantern after you've gathered all the kids together. Some might not be familiar with a fuel-burning lantern, so give them a quick rundown of how it works. Raise the wick so they see how that adds more light.

If you're in a dark enough place, take a short walk with the kids while holding the lantern to demonstrate how it shines light on the path in front of you. You don't want to take much time on this walk. Circle right back to where you started, and you're ready to teach the lesson.

Teaching the Lesson

Campers depend on a good lantern or flashlight when they're out in the wild. The light definitely helps them see what they're doing. It makes things easier and helps prevent mistakes—like when they're setting up a tent in the dark. It also helps them stay on the path if they go out to find firewood. It helps them find their way back home. Campers wouldn't consider leaving their campsite for any reason after dark without taking a light with them.

A good light can also keep campers from walking into danger—or a dangerous situation.

In the Bible, Jesus is described as a light.

When Jesus spoke again to the people, he said, "I am the light of the world. Whoever follows me will never walk in darkness, but will have the light of life." (John 8:12)

The Bible even describes itself as a light.

> Your word is a lamp for my feet,
>   a light on my path. (Ps. 119:105)

How do you think Jesus and the Bible . . .

Keep us from making mistakes?

Make our tasks easier?

Keep us on the right paths?

Keep us from walking into danger?

The Bible also describes Christians as light.

You are the light of the world. A town built on a hill cannot be hidden. Neither do people light a lamp and put it under a bowl.

Instead they put it on its stand, and it gives light to everyone in the house. In the same way, let your light shine before others, that they may see your good deeds and glorify your Father in heaven. (Matt. 5:14–16)

How can we be a light—a good example to others?

How can we help make life easier for others by being a light?

How can we be a light that helps others stay on the right paths?

How can we be a light that helps keep people from walking into danger?

Summing It Up

This is where you need to go someplace really, really dark to finish the lesson. Likely that is indoors. Did you decide to pick up the keychains? Terrific. Bring those with you. This is where you'll use them. DO NOT bring the lantern indoors. Close the door and turn on your pocket flashlight.

Matthew 5 makes it clear that we're to be a light in the world. A light in our own little world. That means we need to be a good example to our friends—and others—of what it means to be a follower of Jesus. We went over some ideas a few minutes ago of what that might look like.

If we are to be a good example to our friends and others, how important is it to be sure *we* are following the light—Jesus—and following the light of his Word?

Sometimes we might think there isn't much we can do to be a good example in a dark world. Hey, we're just one little light, right? But notice how well you can see in here with just this tiny light! I can see each of you clearly.

One tiny light makes a big difference in a dark place. In fact, the darker the spot, the brighter our light will appear. Let's be that

If you bought a little keychain light for each of the kids, this is the time to pull them out and give them to them. Say, "Every time you see your keychain, remember that you're to follow the light, and to be a light to others."

Great job! Be sure to keep spare batteries handy. Replacing the flashlight batteries as needed in the weeks to come is a great way to remind them of the lesson. And as an adult, remember . . . you're a light too. Especially to those kids. Keep your little keychain light handy as a reminder to you as well!

example to our friends—those who are Christians, and those who aren't. Let's be a light in the corner of the world in which Jesus has placed us, okay?

Where Am I?

THEME: We can stop worrying, even when we feel unsure of where we are or where we're headed next. God has a plan—even when we can't figure out what it is.

THINGS YOU'LL NEED

- ☐ Blindfold for each of the kids (a scarf works fine)
- ☐ Paper and pencil for each of the kids

Advance Prep

Map out a route you can drive in about ten minutes or less. On this route you'll need to make three stops. When you do this live with your kids, they'll be blindfolded while you drive. You'll have them lift their blindfold at each stop and give them ten seconds to determine where they are. Your objective for this advance prep is to select stops that will leave the kids confused. You don't want them to know where you're at when they lift their blindfolds.

Be sure to actually drive the route and stop at each stop so you can time it. Even ten minutes will seem like a long time to the kids when they're blindfolded, so if you can keep the route shorter, do that.

Basically, look for spots that the kids may not recognize, especially if they don't see the route you drove to the spot. When I did this with my kids, one of the places I stopped was behind the grocery store. I pulled close to the building—between a dumpster and the loading dock. Because they weren't used to seeing the building from that vantage point, they were confused as to where we were.

Running the Activity

Ideally, do this activity after dark. It will make it harder for the kids to guess where they are when they lift their blindfolds.

When you start out, make sure each of the kids has their blindfold on good so they can't see a thing. And you'll want to be sure each is holding a notebook or paper and a pencil.

You may want to make some extra turns to keep the kids from figuring out where you're going. When you come to the first stop, simply tell them to lift their blindfolds—and they'll have ten seconds to write down where they think they are. Encourage them not to share their answers, because in the end you'll want to see how many each of them got right.

Ten seconds later, make sure they put the blindfolds back in place, whether they wrote anything down or not. You don't want to allow any time extensions here. Proceed to the second stop on your route, and then to the third. Repeat this same procedure each time.

After the third stop, make sure their blindfolds are back on before leaving. You can go home to finish up the lesson around the kitchen table or, maybe better yet, stop at a fast-food restaurant for a snack.

Teaching the Lesson

Have the kids pull out their papers and ask them where they thought you were on the first stop, the second, and the third. All you're looking for is a spot where any one of them couldn't figure out where they were—or maybe a spot they guessed wrong. That's where you'll zero in with a few questions.

When you weren't sure where we were at, were you scared?

Did you feel like wrestling the steering wheel away from me and driving yourself?

Did you feel like jumping out of the car and finding your own way home?

The answer to all of these should be no, *because you* knew where you were going. You *had a plan.*

Perfect! You've set things up beautifully to tie in an important nugget of truth.

You know what, kids? This little drive we took is a lot like the Christian life.

- There will be times in life when you won't know exactly where you are.
- You'll have no idea why you're there.
- You'll have no idea where you're headed next.

This might make us really scared or anxious. Our tendency may be to try to grab control ourselves. Our reaction might even be to try finding our own way. But usually that will end up being a big mistake.

Summing It Up

There will be many times in life when you may find yourself getting scared or anxious. You'll be in a spot that is totally foreign and unfamiliar. You won't know why you're there or where you'll end up next. That can be scary—and can make us worry or even panic.

Remember, God always knows where you are.

> Where can I go from your Spirit?
>> Where can I flee from your presence?
> If I go up to the heavens, you are there;
>> if I make my bed in the depths, you are there.
> If I rise on the wings of the dawn,
>> if I settle on the far side of the sea,
> even there your hand will guide me,
>> your right hand will hold me fast. (Ps. 139:7–10)

Did you notice how these verses point out that he is with you? If you are a follower of Christ, you have his Holy Spirit inside you. God promises that no matter where you are, he'll hang on to you . . . and he'll guide you.

Wow! That is amazingly comforting, isn't it?

> I know that you can do all things;
>> no purpose of yours can be thwarted. (Job 42:2)

God has a plan, and his plans can't be messed up. That's a wonderfully comforting thought as well.

So, when you have those times when you're feeling anxious—not knowing where you really are, why you're there, or where you're headed next—remember our little mystery ride. Remember how you felt today when I was driving.

- You knew I had a plan.
- You knew I wasn't lost.

Remember that God has a plan for us too. He is in control. We can sit back and take a deep breath. Relax. God knows what he's doing and where he's taking us next, even if we don't.

Bottle Rockets and the Meaning of Life

THEME: In this "it's all about me" world, we'd be wise to understand why we really exist.

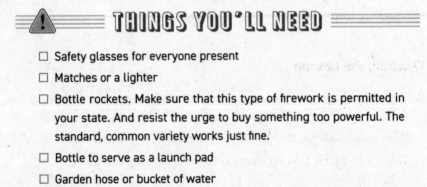

THINGS YOU'LL NEED

- ☐ Safety glasses for everyone present
- ☐ Matches or a lighter
- ☐ Bottle rockets. Make sure that this type of firework is permitted in your state. And resist the urge to buy something too powerful. The standard, common variety works just fine.
- ☐ Bottle to serve as a launch pad
- ☐ Garden hose or bucket of water

Advance Prep

You'll need to find a good, open, clear place to launch the rockets—where there is no risk of them hitting homes, cars, or anything else.

Running the Activity

Talking about the meaning of life may sound like a huge topic for family devotions, but it's an important subject to hit, don't you think?

Start by bringing the kids to the launch site, and make sure everyone is wearing safety glasses—and you have a garden hose or a bucket of water beside you.

Have fun shooting the bottle rockets. If you get a dud that doesn't shoot out of the bottle, be extra safe and douse it with water so there are no accidents.

Some of the bottle rockets will shoot up, leaving a great trail of sparks and ending with a nice report at the end. Others may fizzle out before giving much of an explosion at all. That's all good, so point it out to the kids as it happens. You'll tie that in later.

After you've shot off a bunch of bottle rockets, it's time to get to the lesson. You may want to teach it right there, or grab a snack for everyone to enjoy while you tie it all in.

Teaching the Lesson

Why do you think bottle rockets are manufactured in the first place?

Were they made for the sole benefit of the bottle rockets themselves?
Were they made just so they could have a fun time flying?

Okay, those were ridiculous questions. I think bottle rockets are made for the pure enjoyment of the person launching them—and for those watching them fly. If nobody enjoyed watching bottle rockets, nobody would buy them. If nobody bought them, manufacturers wouldn't make them.

How did you feel about a "dud," a bottle rocket that either wouldn't take off at all or didn't give a nice pop of an explosion at the end? It wasn't all that enjoyable, was it?

So, here's a big question: Why do you think God made us? Why did he make humans like you and me? Is it all about us? Do we exist just so that we can have a great time living our lives . . . simply doing whatever we want to do or feel like doing? Or do you think God made us to bring *him* enjoyment?

> For he chose us in him before the creation of the world to be holy and blameless in his sight. In love he predestined us for adoption to sonship through Jesus Christ, in accordance with his pleasure and will. (Eph. 1:4–5)

> For we are God's handiwork, created in Christ Jesus to do good works, which God prepared in advance for us to do. (2:10)

According to the Bible, God created us for his purposes. He has a plan for us—things he has created us to do. When we live as God created us to live, I imagine that brings him great pleasure.

Summing It Up

Many, many people seem to think their whole purpose in life is to make themselves happy. Their number one priority appears to be pleasing themselves. They seem to feel that life is all about them, without considering the God who made them. When that happens, what kind of people might they become?

- People who are selfish, always looking out for their interests.
- People who are self-focused, thinking mainly about how to please themselves, not God.

If we think more about making ourselves happy than making God happy, how might we be sort of like one of those "dud" bottle rockets?

It's easy to forget that God made us for his enjoyment. But if we keep reminding ourselves why we exist in the first place, we'll make decisions in a whole different way. We'll find ourselves asking, "What will make God happy?" instead of "What will make me happy?"

Congratulations! You've just learned a whole lot about the meaning of life. It's about bringing enjoyment to God. And once we realize that, we can do it more and more, with his help!

So we make it our goal to please him. (2 Cor. 5:9)

As for other matters, brothers and sisters, we instructed you how to live in order to please God, as in fact you are living. Now we ask you and urge you in the Lord Jesus to do this more and more. (1 Thess. 4:1)

So many people chase after happiness their entire life. They find they're never able to stay happy for long. Something is always missing. And it's no wonder. God didn't make us for that kind of life. Those who live to make themselves happy aren't living in a way that matches the whole reason they exist. They're out of tune with why they were created.

Let's remember why we exist. God made us for *his* purposes. God made us to bring *him* glory and enjoyment. God made us to live for *him* . . . not just ourselves. The more and more we live in a way that pleases God, the more we'll realize we were *made* for that. And the good news? When we're living as God designed us to live, chances are we'll find that it truly makes *us* happy too!

Tongue Twisters

THEME: The need to say hard things, like "I'm sorry; I was wrong. Will you forgive me?"

THINGS YOU'LL NEED

☐ Tongue twisters. Pick up a book from the library or print out a number of examples by searching online. A favorite example is Dr. Seuss's *Skipper Zipp's Clipper Ship Chip Chop Shop*.

Advance Prep

Select a few tongue twisters to use with the kids. You don't want to be searching through the book while they are waiting. You'll only need a few examples, so pick a few that will work well for your kids.

Running the Activity

Have the kids read some of the tongue twisters aloud, or, depending on the ages of your kids, let them choose the ones they want you to read. Remember, the tongue twisters need to be read aloud *fast* to illustrate the point.

After you've had some fun reading and stumbling on tongue twisters together, move on to the lesson.

Teaching the Lesson

Tongue twisters are great examples of things that are hard for us to say. But I've got a list of some things that can be even *harder* to say. Would anybody like to try reading them?

- I was wrong.
- It was my fault.
- I'm sorry.
- Will you forgive me?

What is it that makes some of these things so hard to say? Do you think that sometimes it just comes down to pride . . . not liking to admit we're wrong, or even partially wrong? And do you think that sometimes we don't say things like "I'm sorry" because we're so focused on ourselves that we don't notice how we've hurt others—or how our words or actions might impact them?

We need to be aware of how we may be hurting others with things we do and say, don't we? If we aren't treating others right, we aren't living the way God desires us to live. And there are always benefits to living the way God intends us to live.

Therefore confess your sins to each other and pray for each other so that you may be healed. The prayer of a righteous person is powerful and effective. (James 5:16)

Summing It Up

When we've messed up, it's hard to say that we were wrong—and that we're sorry. But that is exactly what we need to do, even if we don't think we're the only one to blame. We have to own the part where we messed up.

If we practiced one of the tongue twisters we read earlier, it would likely get easier and easier to say, wouldn't it? The same thing happens the more we admit when we're wrong—and ask for forgiveness. It will become easier and easier to do that, which will go a long way toward making life a whole lot more enjoyable for us and for those around us.

Be careful to do what is right in the eyes of everyone. If it is possible, as far as it depends on you, live at peace with everyone. (Rom. 12:17–18)

So, let's work on it. Let's say those hard things, like admitting when we do something wrong. Let's say we're sorry when we mess up, even if it only seems like we were a little bit wrong. As we do, we'll have more peace in our lives too. And that's a really, really good thing!

Pure Preserves

THEME: One huge benefit of living a holy life—unpolluted by the world—is that we are actually more appealing to others. Purity is another great theme to teach here.

THINGS YOU'LL NEED

- ☐ Toaster
- ☐ Two slices of bread for toasting
- ☐ Jam/preserves, whatever flavor is a favorite with your kids
- ☐ Plastic sandwich bag filled with dirt collected from a vacuum bag or canister

Advance Prep

When collecting dirt from a vacuum, make sure you get some really nasty-looking stuff. Dust. Dirt. Fuzz. Pet hair. Dried-out bits of food. The more disgusting, the better. Seal a big handful in a clear plastic sandwich bag.

And think about where you want to take this devotional. It's a great one to use to talk about any aspect of living a holy life . . . a life set apart for God. Purity would be an easy fit. You can also use this object lesson to talk about anything that doesn't belong in our lives as Christians. Pride. Selfishness. Greed. Unforgiveness. This is one of those object lessons you can use to illustrate a number of things. Decide if you want to use this to illustrate a bunch of things in general, or if you want to focus in on just one of them.

> NOTE: This devotional can be easily adapted for a powerful talk about purity. If you decide to do so, you'll still run the activity just as described below.

Running the Activity

Ideally, you'll want to do this when your kids are really hungry, perhaps right about that time when they'd love a mid-afternoon snack. Make a couple of pieces of toast and slather them both with a generous helping of jam or preserves—whatever flavor your kids like best. Put each slice on a separate plate, and let the kids inhale the wonderful aroma.

You might ask them if they'd like some. Likely you'll get a positive response. Before you let anyone actually have any, you'll want to pull out the bag of vacuum debris. Dump the whole thing on one of the slices of toast. You may need to use a knife to be sure you spread it over the entire piece. Explain where you got the debris, and let them get a good look at it.

Now ask them which slice they'd like to eat. If you have teenagers, they may pretend to have a hard time deciding. Roll with it . . . and move on to the life lesson.

If the idea of warm toast slathered with fresh jam isn't something that would appeal to your kids, consider swapping it for ice cream with a jam or chocolate topping. Then you'd still add the vacuum dirt just as described. The point of the lesson is still the same. The goal is to be sure you're serving something your kids would really want to eat—until you spoil it with the dirt.

Teaching the Lesson

The toast with the jam looked appealing—really appetizing—until I polluted it with things that didn't belong there. The jam was no longer pure after I dumped the dirt from the vacuum on top.

This is a picture of life. God wants us to be pure, to be holy—like the one piece of toast with the pure preserves on it. God wants us to keep things out of our lives that don't belong there.

> What kinds of things don't belong in a Christian's life but sometimes end up there anyway?
>
> How can things like anger, selfishness, pride, arrogance, unforgiveness, lies, unkindness, pretending to be a better Christian than we are, and a lack of love for others end up polluting our lives?
>
> If we allow things in our lives that don't belong there as Christians, how might that seem unappetizing to someone who doesn't follow Christ? How might that make them want to avoid learning more about Jesus—and what he's done for them? How might it make them totally disinterested in having what we have . . . Christ in our lives?

Jesus died to free us from sin's grip on our lives and from sin's penalty. He doesn't want us to keep living the way we would if we never knew him.

For you were once darkness, but now you are light in the Lord. Live as children of light (for the fruit of the light consists in all goodness, righteousness and truth) and find out what pleases the Lord. Have nothing to do with the fruitless deeds of darkness, but rather expose them. (Eph. 5:8–11)

He wants us to live a life that is pure. He wants us to seek to obey his Word. That is a life that is appetizing—appealing to God and to others.

A Special Word for Parents

If you decided to focus on purity, you might talk about what it means to stay pure in a sexual way. You may need to get specific here. Years ago, we had a president who tried to redefine sex by insisting oral sex is not really sex. Expect that your kids will hear some of that kind of talk from their friends. Help them know where the appropriate boundaries are when it comes to being with a girl or guy before marriage.

You'll want to key in on the fact that friends—or our culture—will want them to believe that adding sex to their lives in some way before marriage will make them more appealing to others. Actually, that isn't true. It is the life that is unpolluted by sin that is more appealing in the long run. For men and women both, those who keep themselves pure and unpolluted will be more appealing to the person they'll want to marry someday. Someone who works to maintain purity is exactly the kind of person the man or woman they will want to spend their life with will also truly desire.

Whenever we're talking about sex and purity, it can be really easy for our kids to misunderstand something we're trying to explain. The topic may make them uncomfortable, and it certainly can make us a little nervous too. Combining those two makes for a formula for miscommunication.

Here are some things you'll probably want to really emphasize. These are so important that you might just want to read them right from the book.

- Sex is not dirty. Sex is a good, good thing. Sex is a very special wedding gift God gives to a man and woman when they get married. This gift is something God wants them to fully enjoy. Sex is one of God's amazing wonders that not only creates life but is designed to draw a husband and wife close—and keep their love intimate and strong. Someday you'll likely get married, and when you do, we want you to enjoy that gift to the fullest too.

- Sex before or outside of marriage is a misuse of God's gift. When we misuse gifts from God, like sex, there will always be negative consequences—often things we can't foresee.

- Having sex doesn't make someone dirty, just like sex itself isn't dirty. But when we disregard God's plan for sex, we allow sin into our lives. Sin doesn't belong in our lives any more than that bag of dirt belongs on that jam.

- When we allow sin into our lives, it always makes a mess we'll deeply regret. When we allow sin in our lives—like having sex before God gives it to us as that wedding gift—it brings emotional pain Mom and Dad don't want you to have to bear. Just like dropping that bag of dust on the jam spoiled that wonderful slice of toast, misusing sex will tragically complicate your ability to enjoy the intimacy of sex in marriage someday—with the very person you'll love more than anyone on earth.

- We want to encourage you to protect that gift God has for you. We want to encourage you to save sex for marriage—the way God designed it to be.

You might also add this verse as you sum things up:

> Flee the evil desires of youth and pursue righteousness, faith, love and peace, along with those who call on the Lord out of a pure heart. (2 Tim. 2:22)

Summing It Up

We all mess up and allow things in our lives that don't belong there. When that happens, we need to confess it to God and ask him to clean us up. We'll probably need to do some confessing and apologizing to others too.

And we can all pray that God will help us avoid the things we should avoid—those things that are not only wrong for us but are worthless. They add nothing to our lives or to eternity. They only take from us. We can ask him to change our hearts so we don't desire wrong and worthless things in our lives. We can pray this verse that we find in the book of Psalms:

> Turn my eyes away from worthless things;
>   preserve my life according to your word. (Ps. 119:37)

We can ask him to preserve our lives, to keep them pure—just like the Bible says we should. Now that life will be really, really appealing!

This would be a great time to make sure everyone gets a snack of fresh toast and jam, if they'd like that. It will be one more way to reinforce the importance of keeping things out of our lives that don't belong there . . . and how that leads to a life that is appealing to others.

The Houdini Principle

The world promotes things that promise to satisfy us, but it's only an illusion.

THINGS YOU'LL NEED

- ☐ A bag of marshmallows. If you have an old bag that is hard and stale, that's even better.
- ☐ Small box, big enough to hold the bag of marshmallows
- ☐ Wrapping paper to wrap the box

Advance Prep

Often when we hear the name Harry Houdini, we think of daring escapes and convincing illusions. Well, you're going to create a bit of an illusion for the kids this week. More importantly, you'll be exposing an age-old illusion: that what the world offers has lasting value and can really satisfy in the long run. That's an important nugget of truth to pass on to the kids, so let's talk about the prep. It's a little more detailed this time, but it's easy . . . and really effective for creating our illusion.

Put the bag of marshmallows in a box, and consider adding something else to give it a bit of weight. A couple of water bottles, maybe? Then wrap the box. Maybe even add a bow to make the present look like there is something of real value inside. Do this several days or even up to a week in advance.

The key is that you want the kids to really, really anticipate opening this mystery present. You want them to buy into the illusion that it contains something wonderful. Valuable. Something they're going to love. To help you give them that impression, here's some ideas.

First, place the present out where the kids can see it for days before the devotional. Let them know you have something really important to share with them this week during your family devotional time. You might tell them there's something in the box for each of them, and they'll get to keep it too. You might tell them you're very excited to give this gift, or that they're finally old enough for you to give this to them—but you can't say any more than that until family devotions.

Next, if you want to really complete the illusion that the box contains something of great value, you might arrange for a relative or family friend to call a few days before the devotional. Put them on speakerphone or video chat so they can say something like this to the kids: "I heard what you're going to get during your family devotions this weekend. I'm so excited for you. Congratulations!"

And if you line up more than one person to make that type of call, keep with the same message but switch it up a little: "I heard about the package you're getting this weekend. You are so lucky!

My parents never did anything like that for me. Call me after you get it. I want to hear all about it."

By this time, the kids are likely all on board. If they're a bit older and wiser, they may be suspicious. That's fine. It will all work to help teach them the important truth of this lesson.

Running the Activity

Get the kids together, and get the camera app on your phone ready. If they see that you intend to record their expressions as they open the package, it will be one last reinforcement of the illusion.

It's time to let them open the mystery box. Now, some kids may get excited about a bag of marshmallows, but older kids are more likely to feel a bit let down—especially with all the buildup you gave it. After their initial reaction, you might make a statement like this to begin the transition toward the nugget of truth: "All week I've been giving you the impression that there was something valuable inside the box. That you were getting something really important. Something you'd really like. Do you feel the marshmallows live up to all the hype I gave it?"

Teaching the Lesson

This is a reminder about how things can be in real life. We're surrounded by ads that give us the feeling or the illusion that they're offering something really valuable. Something that will make life better or more meaningful. Something that will make us happy.

The people who create the ads are good at what they do. They're pros. They can be really, really convincing that the toy or product or vacation spot—whatever they're selling—will make life great.

The thing is, this is really no more than an illusion. But it can be so easy to believe what the world tells us.

- If we get a different friend, life will be better.
- If we get a new phone, we'll be happy all the time.
- If we make the team, get the award, win the role in the play, or whatever, life will change for the better.
- If we get the right education, at the right school, our future will be wonderful.

Even moms and dads fall for the world's illusions all the time.

- If we lose a little weight, we'll be happy.
- If we live in a nicer home, we'll be content.
- If we drive a specific car or truck, life could be so good.
- If we have better jobs and make more money, our problems will melt away.

The thing is, everything the world offers is temporary. It's going to rust or break. Things change.

Do not store up for yourselves treasures on earth, where moths and vermin destroy, and where thieves break in and steal. But store up for yourselves treasures in heaven, where moths and vermin do not destroy, and where thieves do not break in and steal. For where your treasure is, there your heart will be also. (Matt. 6:19–21)

Jesus warns us not to chase after things that really can't satisfy us in the long run. He warns us not to focus on trying to attain more in this life . . . things that won't last for eternity anyway. Instead, he urges us to follow him and go after the things that will matter forever.

Summing It Up

So many people spend their entire life believing the illusion that things of this world can really satisfy them. Sure, maybe those things make people happy for a while, but the happiness will end eventually. Can you imagine how cheated they feel if they don't figure that out until their life is almost over?

If you come to understand that the things of this world really can't make you happy over the long run—and if you live your life for Jesus instead—you'll avoid massive disappointment and regret.

> You make known to me the path of life;
>> you will fill me with joy in your presence,
>> with eternal pleasures at your right hand. (Ps. 16:11)

The paths that lead to true joy and pleasure that never ends? They're the paths that God will lead us on if we follow his Word. Let's be careful not to fall for the illusions the world tries to make us believe. And let's pray that God helps us to see clearly . . . to fully realize that the truly good things in life all revolve around God and around being a true disciple of Jesus.

Laser Lesson

THEME: People—and God—don't invest in us just so we can absorb more but so that we can share with others.

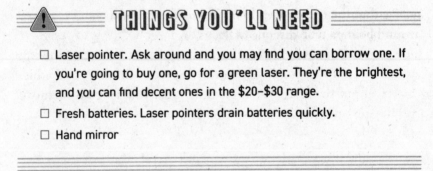

THINGS YOU'LL NEED

☐ Laser pointer. Ask around and you may find you can borrow one. If you're going to buy one, go for a green laser. They're the brightest, and you can find decent ones in the $20–$30 range.

☐ Fresh batteries. Laser pointers drain batteries quickly.

☐ Hand mirror

Advance Prep

The safety icon is included in this lesson simply because of the brightness of that laser. You want to be sure to keep it away from the eyes, okay? You're looking to teach a nugget of truth here, not do laser surgery. Now, test the laser with the hand mirror just to see how easy it is to redirect the beam. You should be able to send the laser beam in an entirely different direction with great accuracy. It's fun, right?

Running the Activity

When turning on the laser, always start with the pointer directed at the floor. Then, watching the laser dot, move it along the floor and direct it toward whatever you want to actually point at. When you first pull out the laser, just have the fun of pointing to different things in the room to showcase the intensity of the beam. If you do this outside at night, point to one of the stars. If you have a green laser in the price range we talked about, it will seem like the laser is going all the way into space. It looks absolutely impressive!

Now you'll want to place the beam right on the shirt of one of your kids. Starting on the floor, work the beam to the one you're targeting, travel up their leg, and hold the laser beam steady on their shirt at about the belly button. If you have one of the kids handling the laser, you'll want to demonstrate the proper/safe way to do this. Once you put the beam on one of the kids, you're ready to move into the next phase of the lesson.

KEEP IT SAFE

Remember, be safe with the laser pointer . . . and make sure you go over some basic safety guidelines with the kids too.

Teaching the Lesson

Imagine that this laser beam represents all the things people do for you. The ways they pour into your lives. Just think about the kinds of things parents and other relatives or family friends do for you. Some take care of you. Make sure you're fed right. Look out for you. Get you to the doctor when you're sick. Protect you in countless ways.

Often the types of things others do for you include teaching you things that you'll need in life. Like how to read and write. How to make smart decisions. And how to stay safe in a dangerous world.

Sometimes the way parents or others pour into your life is by loving you. Forgiving you when you mess up. Being patient with you. Showing mercy even when you may not deserve it. Even pouring truth into you, like right now. All of these are examples of ways that others invest in you.

And when we invest in you, there is something deep down we're hoping will happen. Would anybody like to guess what that might be?

We're hoping that you don't simply keep absorbing all the nice things people do for you, like your shirt is absorbing the laser light. We're hoping you'll give back, and you'll do good things for others too.

Let's demonstrate this.

Now have one kid hold the hand mirror against their stomach, facing downward at a slight angle. Shine the laser at that mirror, and you should see the laser dot on the floor now instead of on their shirt. Ask them to carefully angle the mirror so that the laser dot rests on the shirt of someone else in the room. Depending on the ages of the kids, you might want to add another hand mirror or two and keep the laser going . . . touching more people in the room.

This is a picture of what we hope *you* do. We hope you give back to others. Show others love, mercy, kindness, care, and forgiveness—just like we show you—instead of being content to simply absorb all the good things others do for you.

Do nothing out of selfish ambition or vain conceit. Rather, in humility value others above yourselves, not looking to your own interests but each of you to the interests of the others. (Phil. 2:3–4)

Sometimes we can take all the things people do for us for granted. We may feel we're entitled in some way. That we totally deserve it. Instead, like these verses in Philippians mention, we want to resist that tendency to be selfish or puffed up with some exaggerated sense of self-importance. We want to look for ways to pour into others . . . helping them in ways they need help as well.

Sometimes that will be really hard to do, especially when we don't believe the other person deserves it. Aren't those the times to remember how often people have poured into us, even when we didn't deserve it?

Summing It Up

If we're followers of Jesus, we've been given the greatest gift that can be given. Jesus poured out his own blood—his very life—so that we could have forgiveness of sins and eternal life. We should show some gratitude for that, don't you think? How can we give back, even a little, for the supreme kindness God has shown us in that way? Could we tell our friends about what Jesus did for us? Can we share his love?

I have come into the world as a light, so that no one who believes in me should stay in darkness. (John 12:46)

In a very real way, Jesus shines his light on us. He rescues us from darkness. He shows us mercy and kindness and forgiveness and love. If we're truly grateful for what he does for us, it's pretty clear we need to reflect his love to others. How can we do that?

Pie Face

THEME: How ridiculous we look when we take pride in doing wrong things.

THINGS YOU'LL NEED

- ☐ A pie large enough for each of the kids to get a big slice. Some kind of berry pie would be nice and messy, which is what you want. Be sure you choose a pie flavor your kids will want to eat.
- ☐ Hand mirror. This isn't absolutely necessary, but it will be useful.
- ☐ Optional: whipped cream or ice cream to put on top of the pie, primarily to make it even messier.

Advance Prep

No real advance prep necessary for this one, other than getting the pie.

Running the Activity

Cut the pie into slices and have a piece for each of the kids. Sit them at the table and explain that you're going to have a little pie-eating contest. The first one to finish their pie wins. The catch is that they can't use their hands or any utensils. They'll need to lean in low and eat the pie the way an animal might do it.

Be sure to take pictures as they're eating. And when the race is done, take a close-up of each face before you allow anyone to clean up. Hopefully you're seeing pie up on their cheeks. Likely the winner is pretty proud of themselves. Even after you take the pictures, tell them to wait until after the lesson is done before washing off whatever pie is on their face.

Pass the hand mirror around if you have one. Let each of the kids get a good look at their face. Perfect! You're ready to move on.

Teaching the Lesson

What do you think about how your face looks? What if I didn't let you wipe it off—and then we went to the store or to a restaurant with your face messy like that? What if we went to church that way? What if you went to school that way—or out with your friends? Do you think it might be just a little embarrassing for people to see you looking that messy?

When we make a mess of ourselves, the natural thing to do is to clean up right away, don't you think?

Sometimes we—or friends of ours—make different kinds of messes. Let's imagine someone we know did something that was wrong according to the Bible. Or maybe they talked to or about someone in a way the Bible says we shouldn't. But instead of being ashamed, that person actually felt kind of proud of themselves. The Bible talks about that happening.

For, as I have often told you before and now tell you again even with tears, many live as enemies of the cross of Christ. Their destiny is destruction, their god is their stomach, and their glory is in their shame. Their mind is set on earthly things. But our citizenship is in heaven. And we eagerly await a Savior from there, the Lord Jesus Christ. (Phil. 3:18–20)

"Their glory is in their shame." That means they're actually proud of things they should be ashamed of. You've probably seen this type of behavior before. Sometimes it can even happen to us. Let's brainstorm some examples. (*Here's a list of some things you might bring up—if they're appropriate for your situation or the ages of your kids.*)

- Someone cheats on a test and is proud of their score—even though they didn't earn it.
- Someone may shoplift—and then brag about it to their friends.
- Someone may do something that they know is wrong or unhealthy, but they do it anyway and post about it on some social media platform.
- Someone may lie to their parents—and then brag about how they got away with it.
- Someone may talk back to a parent or teacher—and feel really good about doing it.
- Someone may get involved with another person sexually before they're married—and feel no shame but a sense of victory instead.

What about you . . . can you add some other examples?

Do you see how this is sort of like being a mess—like having a face covered in pie and then going out in public without getting cleaned up? It should be embarrassing. But often we can "glory" in the very things that should embarrass us or make us feel shame.

Summing It Up

Sometimes we need to ask ourselves if the things we glory in would make Jesus proud. If not, maybe we need to ask him to help clean us up. It can be hard because we can have an appetite for things that are wrong. We can ask God to help us . . . to change our hearts and our desires.

> Trust in the LORD and do good;
> > dwell in the land and enjoy safe pasture.
> Take delight in the LORD,
> > and he will give you the desires of your heart. (Ps. 37:3–4)

Sometimes we may forget how wrong some things are in God's eyes. We mess up but forget all about the need to clean up. The Bible is like a mirror, showing us how we look . . . how we measure up to how God wants us to live. That's another reason to read our Bible regularly.

Take a look in that mirror again (*or take them to a bathroom mirror*). Was it hard not wiping off your face, knowing the mess that was there? Would you have felt good going to the store without cleaning up first? Probably not.

We all mess up. We all sin. But we pray that afterward, instead of being proud of what we did, we'll always feel shame and regret. We pray that this will nudge us to repent—to turn from whatever sin we got involved in—and do what we need to do to clean up our mess.

Sometimes we may get ourselves in a mess that is so big, we don't even know where to start when it comes to cleaning up. Confess that to God—and know Jesus can help. And know that you can talk to me—always. I want to help you, and I will.

Speaking of that, I think we've left that mess on your face long enough, don't you? Let's get cleaned up.

The Time and Place
for Extra Space

THEME: Allowing more time for Jesus in our lives.

THINGS YOU'LL NEED

- ☐ Quarters. At least a $10 roll, but more depending on the number of kids present. Figure about $5 in quarters per person. Don't worry, you'll likely get most of it back.
- ☐ Small plastic caps, such as those from plastic milk cartons, juice bottles, or water bottles. Ideally, you'll have one cap for each kid.

Advance Prep

Practice stacking quarters in the caps you've collected so you have a feel for how this works—and so you're reasonably sure you picked up enough quarters. You'll want to put a time limit on this as well. The older the kids, the less time—or they'll earn too many quarters.

Let's say you settle on twenty seconds. You'll want to stack as many quarters in that cap as you can, and walk once around the kitchen table—balancing the entire stack of quarters—all within twenty seconds. Modify the time if you feel the activity will be too easy or too hard. The kids will get to keep the quarters they successfully keep in that stack—without touching it, of course—as long as they get to the finish line within twenty seconds.

Running the Activity

Explain the rules to the kids.

- They stack quarters in their cap.
- They get to keep all the quarters—as long as they don't touch them, the quarters don't fall, and they make it around the table—all within twenty seconds.

Allow one kid to go at a time. Skip the kids who are really too young for this anyway.

Have each of the kids count up how much they earned—and report their total out loud.

Teaching the Lesson

Well, you earned yourself a little money here! Can you imagine how much you might've earned if you'd used something bigger to carry the quarters in instead of a little cap? What if you were able to use a bowl or a bucket? How about a wagon?

And what if we didn't limit the time to twenty seconds? What if you had hours to pile up quarters and make trips around the table?

Can you imagine how much money you would earn if you had all day to pile quarters in the bed of a pickup truck—or in the body of a dump truck? That would definitely give you some serious cash benefits.

> And she gave birth to her firstborn son and wrapped him in swaddling cloths and laid him in a manger, because there was no place for them in the inn. (Luke 2:7 ESV)

This might sound like a strange Bible verse to read at this moment, but there's a point to it. The innkeeper had no room for Jesus. No space. Do you think he ever regretted not giving Joseph and Mary and Jesus his *own* room for the night? For over two thousand years, this innkeeper has been known as the guy who couldn't make room for Jesus in his life. He's often portrayed as kind of a loser, right? Certainly he lost something by not allowing Jesus space. Most people would agree that he made a tragic mistake.

Sometimes we do the same thing, don't we? We can't seem to carve out even a little time for Jesus in our daily lives. And that's even more tragic than what the innkeeper did. The innkeeper didn't know he was turning down God's Son. But when we fail to give Jesus time and space in our lives, we know exactly who we're leaving out in the cold.

Summing It Up

There's a famous story in the Bible about when Jesus came to a home where two sisters lived.

> As Jesus and his disciples were on their way, he came to a village where a woman named Martha opened her home to him. She had a sister called Mary, who sat at the Lord's feet listening to what he said. But

Martha was distracted by all the preparations that had to be made. She came to him and asked, "Lord, don't you care that my sister has left me to do the work by myself? Tell her to help me!"

"Martha, Martha," the Lord answered, "you are worried and upset about many things, but few things are needed—or indeed only one. Mary has chosen what is better, and it will not be taken away from her." (Luke 10:38–42)

Martha wasn't doing bad things with her time. She was doing good things *for* Jesus . . . but she was too busy to spend time *with* Jesus. That can happen to a lot of us as Christians. We can get busy doing things that aren't necessarily bad, but we end up with no time left for Jesus. Sometimes we can even get so busy with church things—doing things for the Lord—that we miss time actually being with him and learning from his Word. Mary made a better choice. She carved out time for Jesus. She gave up some space in her life for him.

If I'd allowed you more time to gather quarters and something bigger to haul them in, you'd be a lot richer right now. That little activity should remind us of how we choose to follow Jesus in our lives. If we give him just a tiny bit of time and a tiny bit of space, likely we'll only see a tiny benefit. But if we give him more? Like Mary, we'll be making a better choice—and we'll be richer in so many ways for doing that!

Shaving Cream Fight

THEME: God, in his great mercy, cleans up our messes.

THINGS YOU'LL NEED

- ☐ Shaving cream—at least two cans for each person. More is better. Get the cheap stuff; it works just fine.
- ☐ Outdoor location to have a shaving cream fight
- ☐ Access to a hose, shower, and supplies for cleanup afterward

Advance Prep

No real advance prep is needed. This would be the time to decide if you'll participate in the shaving cream fight yourself or just run the activity from the sidelines. The best possible scenario might be for you to join the fight. The kids will be excited to have the license to spray Mom or Dad with shaving cream. And if you are actually in the fight, you can help keep it going in the right direction. To best illustrate the point of this lesson, you'll want the kids to be a major mess by the time the shaving cream fight is over.

Running the Activity

Be sure the kids are wearing clothes that are okay to get totally messed up with shaving cream. Take the kids to the backyard or wherever you've decided to have the fight. Set some boundaries. The smaller the space the kids have, the less chance they'll have of escaping the shaving cream attacks on them. Remind the kids to do their best to keep the shaving cream out of each other's eyes. You might tell the kids that when all the shaving cream is gone, you'd like to take pictures of each of them.

Now, let the fight begin.

When the shaving cream is gone, be sure to get plenty of pictures that really show how each of them has become a mess. Close-ups of shaving cream on the face or in the hair would be great too.

Before moving on to teach the lesson, you'll want to get the kids cleaned up. Some shaving cream has that menthol ingredient, which can be an irritant.

To help drive home the theme of the lesson, you'll want to participate as much as possible in actually cleaning the kids up.

1. Hose them down outside.
2. Hand them towels.
3. If kids are young enough that you'd help them with their shower afterward, great. If they are old enough to shower on their own, send them off to take a quick one.
4. Instruct the kids that once they're cleaned up and in dry clothes, you'll all gather back together to teach the lesson.

Teaching the Lesson

Start things off by showing them the photos. You might ask a couple of questions to help transition them to the spiritual truth you want to get across.

- Who do you think ended up being the biggest mess?
- How good did it feel afterward to get cleaned up and back into clean, dry clothes?

There's a story in the Bible that tells of a woman who got messed up—but not with shaving cream. She made a mess of her life with sin.

At dawn he appeared again in the temple courts, where all the people gathered around him, and he sat down to teach them. The teachers of the law and the Pharisees brought in a woman caught in adultery. They made her stand before the group and said to Jesus, "Teacher, this woman was caught in the act of adultery. In the Law Moses commanded us to stone such women. Now what do you say?" They were using this question as a trap, in order to have a basis for accusing him.

But Jesus bent down and started to write on the ground with his finger. When they kept on questioning him, he straightened up and said to them, "Let any one of you who is without sin be the first to throw a stone at her." Again he stooped down and wrote on the ground.

At this, those who heard began to go away one at a time, the older ones first, until only Jesus was left, with the woman still standing there. Jesus straightened up and asked her, "Woman, where are they? Has no one condemned you?"

"No one, sir," she said.

"Then neither do I condemn you," Jesus declared. "Go now and leave your life of sin." (John 8:2–11)

According to the Mosaic law, this woman's sin carried the penalty of death. But Jesus, in an act of mercy, found a way for the woman's life to be saved.

In reality, all of us are in a similar spot as that woman. All of us do wrong things. We sin in all kinds of different ways. Some sin more and some sin less . . . but everybody sins. And that sin makes a mess of our lives. The Bible says that the penalty of sin is death.

> For the wages of sin is death, but the gift of God is eternal life in Christ Jesus our Lord. (Rom. 6:23)

But just like Jesus found a way to show that woman mercy, God has offered a way for us—through Jesus—to be cleansed from our sin. God wants to show each of us mercy in that way.

Even if we are followers of Christ, we're going to mess up sometimes. Let's remember that Jesus wants to show us mercy by cleaning us up.

> If we confess our sins, he is faithful and just and will forgive us our sins and purify us from all unrighteousness. (1 John 1:9)

Summing It Up

How crazy would it have been if you *didn't* want to get cleaned up after the shaving cream fight? And it's the same way in life. When we do wrong things, or say something unkind or untruthful, or whatever way it was that we sinned, we need to confess that right away and ask God to clean us up.

Jesus showed great mercy to the woman in that Bible passage. But he also left her with the warning that she needed to make some changes so that she wouldn't keep sinning. God is merciful, but that doesn't mean we can keep doing wrong things, does it?

After our shaving cream fight, you probably wanted to get in clean, dry clothes—and it felt really good when you did. In the same way, when we make a mess of ourselves, let's confess it and ask Jesus to clean us up. We'll feel a lot better after we do.

Paddle Battle

THEME: Prayer is an essential part of the Christian life—but it only benefits us as we use it.

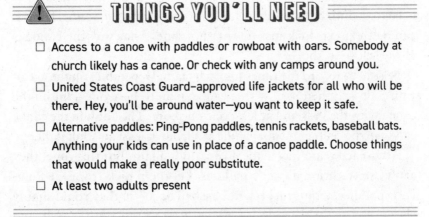

THINGS YOU'LL NEED

- ☐ Access to a canoe with paddles or rowboat with oars. Somebody at church likely has a canoe. Or check with any camps around you.
- ☐ United States Coast Guard–approved life jackets for all who will be there. Hey, you'll be around water—you want to keep it safe.
- ☐ Alternative paddles: Ping-Pong paddles, tennis rackets, baseball bats. Anything your kids can use in place of a canoe paddle. Choose things that would make a really poor substitute.
- ☐ At least two adults present

Advance Prep

All you really need to do is make arrangements to borrow that canoe and gather the other supplies needed.

Another thing to consider is having extra adults present. Don't try this one without at least two adults on-site. You'll be around water, and having more adults present is one way to keep this lesson flowing smoothly and safely all the way. Maybe you can team up with another family. More kids, yes, but you'll also have more adults to keep an eye on safety.

Running the Activity

Have each of the kids put on a life jacket as soon as you get to the water. Make sure each one fits properly, and that the buckles and straps are securely fastened.

You'll be having a race of sorts—just by racing the clock. You can set up teams if you like. But each team is to wear life jackets, get in the canoe, and race from point A to point B and back. There is no need to go into deep water or far from shore with the canoe. Point B can be the next dock just up the shoreline. That way the canoe is always close to shore.

Be sure to record the times for each team. Depending on the age of your kids and their skill with a canoe, plan to have one adult in the canoe with the kids and at least one on shore. The adult in the canoe can sit in the center and not paddle at all, but at least an adult is there.

After each team has made a run, do it again. But this time, they can't use traditional canoe paddles. Let them pick from the Ping-Pong paddles, tennis rackets, or baseball bats—or they could simply choose to use their hands as paddles. Record this time as well, and compare how much longer and harder canoeing became when they weren't using the right tools for the job.

Perfect, you're all set. You're ready to teach the nugget of truth.

Teaching the Lesson

If we had a long way to paddle, had to go upstream against a current, or wanted to get somewhere faster or more efficiently in the canoe, we'd definitely choose the real paddles for the job, right?

In some ways, life is a little like a canoe trip. The canoe will only drift if we don't paddle, and we'll never get where we're supposed to go. And to paddle, God gives us tools for this Christian life. Just like paddles, these tools are designed to help us get where we're supposed to go.

One of the tools he's given us is prayer.

The prayer of a righteous person is powerful and effective. (James 5:16)

Do not be anxious about anything, but in every situation, by prayer and petition, with thanksgiving, present your requests to God. And the peace of God, which transcends all understanding, will guard your hearts and your minds in Christ Jesus. (Phil. 4:6–7)

God gives us prayer. The chance to bring our fears and hurts and needs to almighty God. But sometimes we don't use the tools God designed for us in this Christian life. Sometimes we try other things instead of prayer. Can anybody think of some?

Sometimes we just talk to others. We get advice from friends. That may be okay, but it's never enough. We should be talking to God, too, don't you think?

Sometimes we just attempt to figure out a solution on our own . . . or we try harder. We rely on ourselves somehow. Maybe on our own experience. That's sort of like paddling a canoe with our hands (or a baseball bat, tennis racket, and so on) while the real paddle just sits on the floor of the canoe.

God knows we need to talk to him, to come to him for wisdom—to come to him for strength beyond what we have on our own.

Summing It Up

If we're not used to handling a canoe paddle, it can be awkward at first. It can feel inefficient. It can feel slow. And that's how it can be with prayer too. Prayer is something we get better at the more we do it.

Sometimes we get impatient. We just want to get moving. We want to make something happen. Sometimes prayer can seem like it will take too long. That is sort of the battle of the paddles. We can be tempted to settle for something that is not at all the powerful tool that prayer is. Prayer plugs us in to something beyond us. Something supernatural. The Bible is full of examples of people who prayed . . . and it made all the difference!

Like a canoe paddle for a canoe, prayer is an essential tool for the life God has given us. It takes some time for us to get used to it, but it is well worth it. In the long run, it is the one thing that will help us get where we need to go—or rather to where God wants us to go.

Let's work at learning how to pray. Not just before meals or before bedtime, but all throughout the day.

A Special Word for Parents

You may want to help your kids by teaching them a basic model for prayer. Some like to use ACTS (adoration, confession, thanksgiving, supplication). The Lord's Prayer is a great model for prayer. Walk them through these models so they can see the various elements that make for effective prayer.

This, then, is how you should pray:
"Our Father in heaven,
hallowed be your name,
your kingdom come,
your will be done,
on earth as it is in heaven.

Give us today our daily bread.
And forgive us our debts,
     as we also have forgiven our debtors.
And lead us not into temptation,
     but deliver us from the evil one." (Matt. 6:9-13)

Beauty Is a Beast

THEME: Before dating anyone, we must remember to look beyond surface things—like beauty—if we want that relationship to go the distance.

THINGS YOU'LL NEED

- ☐ Used car lot. Ideally, nothing too big. You don't want the kids overwhelmed with hundreds and hundreds of cars. And you don't want the kids all spread out where you can't keep track of them while they're looking around. Often a new car dealership will have a reasonably sized used car section. That will work perfectly.

Advance Prep

Find a dealer selling used vehicles, and take a walk through that lot. You'll want to get a feel for where the used cars end and the new cars start. You might check their store hours while there. Where I live, car dealerships are closed on Sunday. That's a perfect time to bring the family. The lot is open—because they want people to browse. But there won't be a sales force present asking you questions.

Maybe you're wondering about doing this one. *Isn't it too early to talk about dating? They're not nearly old enough to date.* I hear you. But that's the ideal time to talk about this topic because the issue won't be so emotionally charged. Remember, your kids are getting all kinds of messages from the world about the kind of person they should date someday. To really help and protect your kids, you'll need to balance that out with perspective and truth from God's Word.

This lesson becomes much harder to teach when your kids are ready to date—or have their eyes on somebody. You'll feel like you're playing defense. So teach this lesson before the kids are of dating age, and you'll be playing offense. You'll be making a preemptive strike.

Running the Activity

Take the kids to that used car lot. Invite them to take ten minutes to look through the used cars and trucks. Their goal is to choose one that they'd pick today if money was no object. You can assure them that you're not actually going to buy anything today, but you'd like to see what they'd want you to purchase, if you were. Then, when the ten minutes are up, they'll bring you to the vehicle of their choice and tell you why they picked it.

Find a place to stand where you can keep an eye on all the kids, especially if you have more than one. Hold off from giving any advice or editorial comment while they're making their decisions. Once the time is up—or they've made their choice—gather the kids back together.

Now, give each of them a turn to lead the entire family to the car or truck they chose. Ask them to explain why they selected that vehicle. Take a picture of them with their dream car or truck.

Once everyone has shared, pack them up in the car and go home—or to a fast-food place—to teach the lesson. Getting kids a snack is always a great way to help keep their attention.

Teaching the Lesson

Let's review some of the reasons you picked the specific car or truck that you chose. *You'll want to recap some of the actual input you got from your kids.*

If I had a typical group of high schoolers here, and we did the same activity, what kinds of things might have made them choose a particular vehicle?

- Some might choose based on color, vehicle model, or brand.
- Some might choose based on looks . . . they like every line and curve of that vehicle.
- Some might choose the most expensive car or truck they could find.
- Some might choose a vehicle that was really fast or looked really cool.
- Some might choose a vehicle based on what would make their friends jealous.
- Some might pick an electric vehicle—something economical or environmentally friendly.
- Some might choose based on the features.
- Some might choose based on how good they believe having that vehicle will make them feel.

All these factors may influence someone's decision, but they're all kind of surface issues, aren't they? All the vehicles we saw are used. Sure, they looked great on the outside, but if we want a car or truck to last, to go the distance, what do we really need to know?

We'd need to know how the engine was, right? If we were really buying, we'd want a mechanic to take a look under the hood to make sure the things that really drive that vehicle are mechanically sound, like the motor and the transmission.

In life, we can make some pretty big decisions based on our emotions—what we like or what makes us feel good. When it comes to the person we'll date or marry, often we base our decisions on a person's outward appearance. That's really, really dangerous. That's one way beauty can be kind of a beast. We can put such a priority on a person's outward appearance that we overlook the most important things, like the condition of their heart. Making "looks" such an important part of the decision can lead to bad choices that will tear us apart later.

Check out this verse from the Bible that talks about an inner quality in a person that is a type of beauty that lasts:

> Charm is deceptive, and beauty is fleeting;
>> but a woman who fears the LORD is to be praised.
> (Prov. 31:30)

And in this verse, we see how God emphasizes the importance of the heart of a person, not just their looks:

> But the LORD said to Samuel, "Do not consider his appearance or his height, for I have rejected him. The LORD does not look at the things people look at. People look at the outward appearance, but the LORD looks at the heart." (1 Sam. 16:7)

Summing It Up

When choosing our dream vehicles, nobody said, "This is the one I think I'd choose—but only after a mechanic had a good look at the things I can't see." Nobody said that, but wouldn't it have been a good idea?

It's the same when we're talking about dating. We can get so wrapped up with how a person looks or how they make us feel. But what do we really need to know? The condition of their heart.

Where is that person in their relationship with Jesus?

How dedicated are they to obeying God's Word, even when they don't feel like it?

Are they serious about loving God and loving others, the things Jesus described as the two most important commandments? How do we see that play out in their life—or is it just talk?

What kind of "fruit" is coming from their life? The kind the Holy Spirit produces?

Are they proud, selfish, or unforgiving?

Are they kind?

These issues, and more, are pretty important when making a decision about someone we date. We might fall in love with that person and end up marrying them. If we make a bad decision about a car, we can always sell it and find a new one. It doesn't work that way with marriage. Marriage is for keeps. You want to make sure the person you marry is a true disciple of Jesus. One who will be true to him—and to you—for a lifetime. A person with the kind of heart that will go the distance with you that way.

Who is the one who truly knows our hearts . . . and every other person's heart? God. And if God is the one who truly knows each person's heart, doesn't it make sense to stay close to him? We can ask him to keep us from being so focused on the surface stuff. We can ask him to reveal the person—one with the right heart—he'd want us to fall in love with. And we can ask him to help us become the person we should be for them too.

A Special Word for Parents

Okay, parents, can you see why this is so important? If your kids are in middle school, do this lesson. Certainly you'll want to do this if they're in high school. When we did this with our boys, one of our nieces tagged along. She was in elementary school, but years later she referred to that trip to the car lot and the lesson behind it. She remembered—even after all those years—and it had influenced her. Don't avoid this one, okay? You'll be helping your kids prepare for their future. Good job!

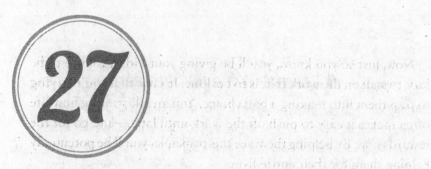

No Sweat

THEME: Laziness and procrastination may be common, but they're not good . . . and not things God rewards.

THINGS YOU'LL NEED

☐ Outline a couple of age appropriate chores or jobs for your kids to do. Ideally, things your kids can handle on their own, without your supervision. Washing the car. Vacuuming. Washing the floor. Cleaning the bathroom.

Advance Prep

Get the supplies ready for whatever job you'll have the kids do: bucket, sponge, hose, towels, and so on. I'm going to go through the rest of this lesson as if washing the car is the job you've chosen for the kids to tackle.

Now, just so you know, you'll be giving your kids a chance to be lazy, to stall on the work that is to be done. It's not that you're trying to trap them into making a bad choice. You are illustrating how life often makes it easy to push off the work until later—and go for the rewards now. By helping them see this principle, you'll be potentially helping them for their entire lives.

Running the Activity

Get the kids together and tell them you have a job for them to do. Show them the supplies you've collected and tell them that when they've finished, they'll get a reward. It's really important that you show them the supplies— everything they'll need to do the job. And it's essential to choose a reward they'd actually like. Go out for ice cream or for pizza? Go to the park or on some other fun outing—or to catch a movie? You decide . . . but you'll want to choose something your kids will be champing at the bit to do.

Now, after they see the supplies—and you tell them about the reward they'll get afterward—offer them the chance to get the reward now. It will be their choice.

- They can do the work first—then go for the reward.
- Or they can have the reward—and then come home to do the work.

If they choose to do the work first, you ought to be a mighty thankful parent. Many kids wouldn't choose that option. But if that is where your kids are at . . . great. As you teach the lesson, just adapt it a bit. I'll be sharing the lesson as if they chose to get the reward first.

Now, if the kids have chosen the reward first (which I'm guessing they will), reinforce things one more time. "Okay, you're choosing to get the reward first. Then you'll do the work after you've had the reward, agreed? I won't have to remind you to do it . . . and you'll do it right away when we get home. Is that it?"

If they agree to that, perfect. You're all set. Take them out for that reward. And when you come home, hold up your phone and mention that you need to take care of something that can't wait. Now disappear without mentioning a word about washing the car. Retreat to your bedroom or someplace where they don't see you around.

Give them fifteen or twenty minutes. Then come back.

- Are they working on the car? Wow . . . time to thank God.
- Are they busy doing other things? No worries, they're doing what most kids would do. And it's your job to kindly train them not to be like most kids, right?

Teaching the Lesson

Gather them together. If they've started washing the car, you can wait until they finish. If they haven't started, dig right into the lesson.

I notice that you haven't even started washing the car, yet before we went for the reward, you assured me that you'd start all on your own as soon as we got back.

Likely there will be plenty of excuses . . . but that's all they are. If you were careful to have all the supplies ready, and you made the deal beforehand that they'd start all on their own, they don't have much to stand on.

Kids, this is a lot like life. All of us want the rewards that come from hard work, but often we choose to take the rewards without the work, if we can. People tend to want the benefits without putting in the sweat.

When we stall on doing work or things that need to be done, that's called procrastination. When we avoid work—or don't put in much effort—that's just being lazy. We can come up with lots of excuses for why we don't do the work. Usually it still boils down to that one character trait . . . being lazy.

Worse, often our human nature still wants or expects the rewards—even though we haven't done the work to earn them.

Some people do that with credit cards. They charge something on a credit card—even though they don't have the money for it. They figure that they'll work off the debt later.

Some people do that with their jobs. "Give me a pay raise now, and then I'll show you what I can do," they say.

In both cases, people can get in the habit of getting the reward first and doing the work later. That can lead to all kinds of debt. And it can lead to loss, resulting in us missing something we could've had if we'd worked a little harder for it up front. In the case of a job, often the person who demonstrates great work habits all the time will get offered the promotion, not the one who promises to work harder *after* the promotion.

God doesn't generally operate on a "rewards first, work later" basis. It can be easy to talk about being a good worker, but the real payoff comes from actually *being* a good worker.

> All hard work brings a profit,
>> but mere talk leads only to poverty. (Prov. 14:23)

In the name of the Lord Jesus Christ, we command you, brothers and sisters, to keep away from every believer who is idle and disruptive and does not live according to the teaching you received from us. For you yourselves know how you ought to follow our example. We were not idle when we were with you, nor did we eat anyone's food without paying for it. On the contrary, we worked night and day, laboring and toiling so that we would not be a burden to any of you. We did this, not because we do not have the right to such help, but in order to offer ourselves as a model for you to imitate. For even when we were with you, we gave you this rule: "The one who is unwilling to work shall not eat." (2 Thess. 3:6–10)

Summing It Up

When we are slow to get work done, or we need to be reminded over and over to do our work, that is procrastinating—or just being lazy. And those are *not* good things.

Instead, whatever it is that you have to do, get it done . . . and do a good job at it. Don't put it off. These verses in Colossians remind us to think of ourselves as working for Jesus. Whatever job we need to do, we also need to realize that he is the one who will ultimately reward us.

Whatever you do, work at it with all your heart, as working for the Lord, not for human masters, since you know that you will receive an inheritance from the Lord as a reward. It is the Lord Christ you are serving. (Col. 3:23–24)

If you do that, you will stand out from so many others. That is a reward too, because you'll develop a good reputation . . . something that is of huge value.

A good name is more desirable than great riches;
to be esteemed is better than silver or gold. (Prov. 22:1)

So, show of hands: Who wants to work at fighting the tendency to procrastinate or be lazy? Good. Because right now, you have a car to wash!

Paintballs and Prayer

THEME: The importance of praying, even if we think God has already decided what he's going to do.

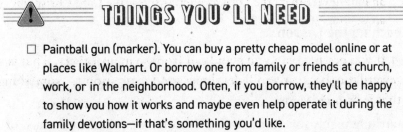

THINGS YOU'LL NEED

- ☐ Paintball gun (marker). You can buy a pretty cheap model online or at places like Walmart. Or borrow one from family or friends at church, work, or in the neighborhood. Often, if you borrow, they'll be happy to show you how it works and maybe even help operate it during the family devotions—if that's something you'd like.

- ☐ Paintballs; select a color you'll be able to match at the paint store.

- ☐ Safety glasses for everyone

- ☐ Plywood (up to 4' x 4') to use as a target

- ☐ Paint that matches the paintball color. You'll be painting one side of the plywood a dead ringer to the color of your paintballs.

Advance Prep

If you're borrowing or buying a paintball gun, you'll want to test all of this gear on your own so you're familiar with how to use it.

Also, pick up the paint to match the paintball color, and use it to paint only one side of the plywood.

Running the Activity

Get the kids together, go over basic safety instructions, and make sure everyone wears their safety glasses. Now let each of them have a turn shooting a handful of shots at the *unpainted* side of the plywood target.

Next, flip the plywood around and let them each take a few shots at the painted side.

Then move on to teach the lesson—even though they probably want more turns to shoot. You can let them have more fun shooting later, but you want to get to the heart of this before they tire of the activity.

Teaching the Lesson

Which side of the target was more fun to shoot at, the side that was painted the same color as the paintballs—or the side that wasn't?

It was harder to see the results when we shot at the side with the matching paint, wasn't it? And if we don't seem to notice much of a difference when we shoot, is it easier to quit shooting?

It can be similar with prayer. Sometimes we shoot prayers up to God—and we really can't see any results. No real change. That could make it easier to give up and stop praying. Maybe, when we think about praying, we wonder what the point even is. If we can't always see the results, and we think God probably has already decided what he's going to do, why bother praying?

This is a hard question, so let's take a look at some verses from the Bible.

And pray in the Spirit on all occasions with all kinds of prayers and requests. (Eph. 6:18)

Rejoice always, pray continually, give thanks in all circumstances; for this is God's will for you in Christ Jesus. (1 Thess. 5:16–18)

You desire but do not have, so you kill. You covet but you cannot get what you want, so you quarrel and fight. You do not have because you do not ask God. When you ask, you do not receive, because you ask with wrong motives, that you may spend what you get on your pleasures. (James 4:2–3)

Just by looking at these verses, we begin to see that prayer is really important. Jesus spent a lot of time praying—and he tells us we need to do that too. That's a good enough reason to do it right there.

Summing It Up

There are things we may not understand—but that doesn't stop us from using them. Like electricity. I may not understand all the science behind what happens when I flip a switch, but that doesn't stop me from using lights. Or think about phones. I may not understand all the technology required to let me hear someone's voice hundreds of miles away, but that won't stop me from using my phone. Prayer can be similar, in a way. Even if we don't always understand why we get answers sometimes and other times we don't, we still need to pray. Even if we might think God already has his mind made up as to what he will do, it still is essential to talk to him about the things on our hearts.

Why does God still want us to pray? Here are several reasons:

- **Prayer focuses our attention on God.** It reminds us that we need his wisdom instead of just relying on our own opinions.

- **Prayer focuses our requests.** What is it we're really asking God for? Putting it into words helps us crystallize our thoughts—or, more importantly, causes us to think things through again. That often opens the door for us to consider how God may see our request, or what his perspective may be on the matter.

- **Prayer exercises our faith.** It takes faith to pray. And as we do, we'll see how God chooses to answer us, one way or another. The Bible tells us to pray regardless of how we feel. Do we believe we should pray? Will we trust him enough to pray—even if we don't see the point? As we exercise our faith, we'll grow stronger in that area.

- **Prayer allows God to work in us.** Sometimes God will show us that our hearts aren't right, and he can change our hearts as a result. Often, as we pray he is preparing us for his answer.

It can be easy to think prayer doesn't make a difference. To think that God will do what God is going to do—regardless of whether we pray or not. But the thing is, if we don't pray, God likely won't be able to grow us and change us and mature us as he'd like to do.

If we don't pray, God likely won't do some of the things *for* us that he'd like to do. Remember the verses in James we read a few minutes ago? Sometimes the only reason we don't have some of the things we feel we need is because we fail to ask God with the right motives. Sometimes we're just plain selfish when we ask God for things. And God likely isn't going to reward us when we're selfish, is he? There are other times that God would like to do the very things we feel we need him to do, but he's just waiting for us to ask so he can strengthen our faith with his answer.

It's more fun to shoot a paintball gun and see the results clearly and immediately. And certainly it would be nice if prayer was always like that—with results that are immediate and easy to see. But whether God answers our prayers quickly and clearly or not, he tells us to pray. And we can be sure that our praying makes a difference. Often, it is the first step toward God making us stronger—and into the very people he has designed us to be.

Some Things ARE Black-and-White

THEME: God's Word gives us some absolute boundaries for right and wrong.

THINGS YOU'LL NEED

- [ ] A key to a locker, lockbox, or maybe a safe-deposit box. Lockers are harder to find these days, but that makes a nice option. Maybe you've got one of those fireproof lockboxes at home. That'll work. Somebody in your family likely has a safe-deposit box—and they'd be willing to go with you and the kids to the bank for that part of the devotional. Or maybe *you've* been thinking of renting a safe-deposit box at the bank. Here's your opportunity.
- [ ] Gift card for a fast-food restaurant your kids like

Advance Prep

Lining up the lockbox, locker, or safe-deposit box is the big thing here. You'll want to get that gift card and place it in an envelope with the kids' names on it. Drop that in the lockbox in advance too.

Whether you use a lockbox, locker, or safe-deposit box, likely you'll find a number stamped onto the key that matches the locker or box. Perfect. You're all set.

Running the Activity

Show the kids the key for the lockbox, locker, or safe-deposit box. Also show them the number on the key and note that this key is designed to open one lock, and one lock only.

If you're using a key from a lockbox you have at home, you might have them try the key in the front door—or any other locks around the house—just to show that it won't open them. If you're at a place with other lockers, you might have them try the key in some of the other locks. Now, use the key to open the correct locker or lockbox.

When they see the envelope inside with their names on it, tell them that they'll get to open it after you talk about the lesson a bit.

Teaching the Lesson

The thing is, we get it. This key is designed to open one lock—and this lock is made to be opened by only one key. It's a black-and-white issue. An absolute. If locks were made to be opened by many, many different keys, there'd be no point to locking things up.

While we get that there is one key for this locker, sometimes we can get fooled into thinking that the Bible doesn't have any areas that are black-and-white—that there are lots of ways to interpret every part of the Bible.

The following is a list of some examples you may give, but add or delete things according to what is age appropriate for your family, okay? And if you have multiple ages present, don't bring this down to the level of your younger kids. Your older ones will check out—and you may not get them back. Your older kids are closer to the big dangers in life, and you have less time with them. Be sure you're keeping the teaching at their level. You can explain a bit more to the younger ones after you're done.

The Bible says we're not to lie (Col. 3:9), but is it okay sometimes, if we really believe we have to?

The Bible says that we're not to go to bed angry (Eph. 4:26), but instead we must deal with the issue or talk it out so we don't keep carrying that anger. But that's more of a suggestion, don't you think? Can God really expect us to do that all the time?

The Bible says that instead of simply doing whatever we feel like doing, we're to exercise self-control, and it makes it clear that living otherwise is sin (2 Tim. 3:1–5). But God doesn't really expect us to live that way all the time, does he?

The Bible says being selfish, unforgiving, or proud is sin (Ps. 101:5; Matt. 18:21–35; Phil. 2:3–4). But don't you think what God really means is to do our best to keep these out of our lives? It's probably okay if we have a little bit of these, because God understands that we're only human, right?

The Bible says we're not to argue or complain (Phil. 2:14–16), but what if we feel something just isn't fair? Surely that's a different story.

Sex before marriage is something the Bible forbids (1 Cor. 6:18–20; Gal. 5:19–21; Col. 3:5–10; 2 Tim. 2:22), but we can't be expected to really live by that anymore, can we? (*I put some extra references here because God's Word is being explained away and watered down so much in this area, even among Christians.)*

The Bible may state some things as being "wrong" (Gal. 6:7–10), but God is loving and gracious. Doesn't that probably mean he'll give us a hall pass on sin—as long as we don't go overboard? And as long as we love others, won't God agree we can do pretty much what we want?

The Bible says we're to treat even our enemies with love (Rom. 12:17–21), but it really depends on the situation, don't you think? If they hold different views than we do, or yell at us, surely there's no reason why we can't dish it right back out to them.

We could go on and on. Our world pushes back against what the Bible says. It discounts the truth of God's Word. Even other Christians—and some pastors and leaders in the church—will often try to soften the boundaries the Bible gives us. They'll give some convincing reasons why the Bible is simply not to be taken "so literally." I suspect they're secretly trying to justify their own disobedience in that area. For whatever reason, they just refuse to accept that there is only one way to interpret what the Bible clearly says—and they want to convince others to believe that as well. But wouldn't they have no problem accepting the fact that a key is made to only fit one lock, not multiple locks?

Summing It Up

When we discount the commands and teachings of the Bible in a way that there are no absolute "right and wrongs," we breed chaos and confusion . . . and eventually a lot of hurt and regret. And the same thing happens when we interpret the Bible in a sloppy way. Like when we aren't accurate with what the Bible really says, or when we try to make it say something it doesn't.

I want to encourage you to read the Bible and realize how black-and-white it is. And when a Christian—even a pastor or a church leader—seems to soften God's commands or give a different interpretation other than what appears to be the obvious meaning? Beware. Read the Bible for yourself. Test what others tell you. God gives us boundaries. To go beyond them is sin, and we'll just end up hurting ourselves. And that is something we definitely don't want.

> How can a young person stay on the path of purity?
>   By living according to your word.
> I seek you with all my heart;
>   do not let me stray from your commands.
> I have hidden your word in my heart
>   that I might not sin against you. (Ps. 119:9–11)

I want to encourage you to stay on the right paths. To live according to what the Bible actually says, even though people will try to tell you the Bible certainly isn't that harsh. Ultimately, we want to live in a way that avoids sin and pleases God.

Just like we saw that there was one key to fit one lock, we know we must be careful to interpret the Bible the right way—the way God intended. We can't just twist his truth to mean whatever we'd like it to mean.

> Do your best to present yourself to God as one approved, a worker who does not need to be ashamed and who correctly handles the word of truth. (2 Tim. 2:15)

When we interpret God's Word the right way, and with God's help we obey what it tells us, it brings so many rewards for this life—and the life to come. Now, let's open that envelope.

The kids should get the gift card. And once they do, it would be great to take them to that place for that meal or snack right away, and once you're there, give them the following reminder.

When we interpret the Bible rightly, it's like putting the right key in the right lock. And as we do, there will certainly be rewards for us. Our lives will be better for it.

Fire Drill

THEME: Keys to escaping temptation.

Advance Prep

If you need to install smoke detectors, do it. If batteries need replacing, get it done.

Work out various plans for how, in case of a fire, you and the family would escape the house from different rooms—and with various scenarios of where the fire actually is. If you picked up an emergency-escape chain ladder, you'll want to test it out in advance with another adult.

Running the Activity

Get the kids together and explain that you're going to talk a bit about fire safety. You might mention that you just installed new smoke detectors (or new batteries in the detectors). Ask two questions:

Why is a smoke detector so important? (It provides an early warning.)

Why is it so important to get early warning of a fire in the home? (It increases the odds of getting out safely, before our exit is blocked.)

Now, run through a series of "fire escape" scenarios, at least half a dozen—and not all of them easy. The most effective way to do this is to actually go to the different spots in the house. If you have a second floor, that brings a whole different set of challenges. Did you pick up a chain ladder designed for escaping a fire from the second floor? Excellent. Now is the time to use that. You can say something like, "Obviously, from a second story, going down the stairs is the obvious choice for getting out of the house. But what if the stairway is in flames that are too big to run past?"

Show the kids the chain ladder and how it works. When we did this for our family devotions, we actually let the kids escape the "burning house" with the ladder. Be sure to have an adult spotter on the ground and one at the window upstairs to help keep everything safe.

If you actually run through this—letting the kids go down the ladder—the devotional will be that much more memorable. And that means they'll remember the point of this lesson too, which goes far beyond fire safety.

Once you've run through the various escape scenarios, you're ready to teach the lesson. Good job!

Teaching the Lesson

It's important that we know how to get out of a burning building or house. Our lives could depend on it. And I think we've seen that there's always a way to escape a fire if we get an early warning—and get out of the house immediately.

There's another kind of fire that can be just as deadly. That fire is temptation. There are all kinds of temptations that can trap us and burn us if we don't escape them quickly. Just like we have early-warning devices and escape plans for a real fire, we can do similar things to keep safe from the fires of temptation.

The Bible is like a smoke detector. It warns us of things to watch out for. It reveals when we're flirting with temptation. It gives us warnings about doing wrong, compromising, lusting, looking at things we shouldn't, having premarital sex, and more.

God has also made Mom and Dad like smoke detectors. We have lived longer and have seen more cases when temptation has burned someone. We try to keep temptation from you whenever we can, but it will come. Sometimes it even comes because, deep down, people actually long for things that are wrong.

> When tempted, no one should say, "God is tempting me." For God cannot be tempted by evil, nor does he tempt anyone; but each person is tempted when they are dragged away by their own evil desire and enticed. Then, after desire has conceived, it gives birth to sin; and sin, when it is full-grown, gives birth to death. (James 1:13–15)

Sometimes people put themselves in danger. Like anyone else, sometimes you will keep thinking about something you want, even though you know it's wrong. It's important to be open with us and to tell us what is going on in your life. What you're struggling with. The idea of talking about those things can be hard. We get that! But it can also be so good for you. Sometimes we smell "smoke" and can warn you—and even help you get out of situations before you get "burned" or hurt in some way.

Sometimes the best escape plans are our own convictions. Believing God's Word and clinging to it tightly. Refusing to let go of it. Staying far from the things that have the power to tempt us.

> Hold on to instruction, do not let it go;
>   guard it well, for it is your life.
> Do not set foot on the path of the wicked
>   or walk in the way of evildoers. (Prov. 4:13–14)

Speed is an issue, isn't it? When the smoke detector first goes off, that is the time to run. There's always a way out—as long as we escape early. With every second we wait, we increase our chances of getting burned. The same thing happens with temptation.

> So, if you think you are standing firm, be careful that you don't fall! No temptation has overtaken you except what is common to mankind. And God is faithful; he will not let you be tempted beyond what you can bear. But when you are tempted, he will also provide a way out so that you can endure it. (1 Cor. 10:12–13)

God promises to provide an escape route when we're tempted—and like a smoke detector, usually his warning comes early. We can't stand around when that happens. We need to move. We need to get away from the temptation, pronto. Or sometimes we need to open up to Mom or Dad right away and tell them about what we're struggling with.

Summing It Up

The Bible gives stories of people who ran from danger when they faced temptation (like Joseph in Genesis 39:11–12) and those who got burned because they didn't (like David in 2 Samuel 11 and the unnamed man in Proverbs 7).

Temptation comes in so many forms. We get tempted to cheat. Lie. Tell only half-truths. Let me encourage you to have an exit plan, a way to escape—a plan to run from temptation. You probably have a pretty good idea of the kinds of temptation that are hard for you to resist. The next time you begin to get tempted in that area, how can you get away from it quickly? Lay out a scenario for escaping from each of the ways you are typically tempted.

If we were running out of the house right now, likely one of us would have our phone. When we got outside, we'd call 9-1-1 and get the fire department on their way to help us. Don't forget that when facing temptation, we need to run—and while we're doing that, we can also send up a 9-1-1 prayer to God for help!

One last thing to think about: Is there a specific temptation you're struggling with right now—or something that regularly tempts you?

A Special Word for Parents

This last question may not get any response at the moment. Likely it is the wrong time to ask it. But do plan to speak with each of the kids privately to ask them the question again. Sometimes the best time to do this is at bedtime, in a darkened room where they don't have to look you in the eyes. If they do talk about a temptation they're struggling with—or have fallen to—remember, be very careful in how you respond. If you respond with anger, likely they'll think twice before sharing honestly with you again. If they've fallen to temptation, your goal is to help treat their burns—and help keep them from falling and being burned again.

The Trouble with Susan B.

THEME: When we live too much like the world, other people fail to see the value of following Christ themselves—or the difference it can make in their lives.

THINGS YOU'LL NEED

- ☐ A handful of change, including at least two quarters
- ☐ At least two old Susan B. Anthony dollar coins. One for each of the kids would be even better. You can check at your bank; sometimes they have some around. Or you can go to a local coin shop and get them cheap—because they aren't all that collectible. They were only made for a handful of years: 1979–81, and then again in 1999.
- ☐ An older silver dollar. You're looking ideally for the Peace type, minted from 1921–28, primarily. You can buy this coin at a local coin shop. It would be great to get one for each of the kids, but if the cost is too high, get at least one as an example. And you don't have to get one in great condition. A more common, beat-up coin is fairly cheap, but

it will still make the point perfectly. If the coin shop angle is out of the question, ask around at church or work. Someone will have one you can borrow.

☐ Blindfold—a scarf will work just fine

Advance Prep

No advance prep other than getting the coins described above.

Running the Activity

1. Have the kids gather around a table, and dump out the handful of change so they all can see it.
2. Keep the Susan B. Anthony coins out of sight but close for an easy grab.
3. Definitely keep the old Peace silver dollar hidden for now.
4. Explain that you'll blindfold one of them, then do so.
5. Ask the blindfolded kid to hold both hands out, palms up, so you can put a coin in each hand. At this point, tap the pile of coins so they hear movement there, but instead of taking coins from the pile, dig the two Susan B. Anthony dollars out of hiding. Place one Susan B. Anthony coin in each palm.
6. Now ask them to close their fists tight around the coins, and say "I put the same size coin in each hand to make this easier for you. Can you guess what coins you're holding?"
7. The odds are really high that they'll guess they're holding the quarters. Perfect. Invite them to remove the blindfold and check their guess.

Now, of course, they'll realize they guessed wrong. Congratulations, you're doing great. You're perfectly positioned to move on with the lesson.

Teaching the Lesson

At first it seemed like you were holding quarters, but in reality you were holding Susan B. Anthony dollar coins. And that was the problem with those Susan Bs. People were always mistaking them for quarters. It was annoying. The Susan Bs are really close to the same size as quarters, and they have the same grooved edges. The government simply stopped making them. I imagine they learned that it's really important for a dollar coin to be quickly seen as different from a quarter.

Sometimes we have a similar problem with followers of Christ. Let's imagine that Christians are dollar coins, and those who are not following Christ are quarters. I'm not saying that Christians are more valuable, but there certainly is value to being a Christian, isn't there?

What are some things Christians have that people without Christ don't?

- We have forgiveness from our sins.
- We have eternal life.
- We have the Holy Spirit working in us and through us to bring us things like peace, love, joy, self-control, and more . . . all in supernatural ways.
- We have God's promise that he will never leave us or forsake us.
- We are adopted as children of the King and can go to our Father in prayer at any time.
- We have God's promise that he will lead us and guide us as we acknowledge and look to him.
- We have God's promise that he will make good things come from even the hard things in our lives.

We could go on, right? But I think we get the point. Christians have things of value that the world does not have.

But all too often, people who don't have a relationship with God through Christ don't see any real difference between how they live and how Christians live.

- Christian siblings still argue and fight and sometimes say they hate each other.
- Christian kids still mouth off to their parents and complain about them to their friends.
- Christian kids still lie and cheat and say unkind things to others.
- Christian kids still hold grudges.
- Christian kids worry and fret just like kids who don't have Jesus.
- Christian kids sometimes live one way at home and a different way with friends or at school.
- Christian kids sometimes do the very things the Bible tells them not to do . . . but they hide them instead of dealing with them.

Again, we could go on, but you get the idea. The more we live like the world lives, the less people see the value of following Christ.

Let me show you what silver dollars used to look like. *Pass that Peace dollar around along with a Susan B. Let them feel the weight. The difference between the two.*

If I put one of these old silver dollars in your hand, you would never have mistaken it for a quarter. And that is the way it should be with us as Christians. We are to be different from the world . . . in good ways.

For the grace of God has appeared that offers salvation to all people. It teaches us to say "No" to ungodliness and worldly passions, and to live self-controlled, upright and godly lives in this present age, while we wait for the blessed hope—the appearing of the glory of our great God and Savior, Jesus Christ, who gave himself for us to redeem us from all wickedness and to purify for himself a people that are his very own, eager to do what is good. (Titus 2:11–14)

Our whole lives, the things we do and say, the way we think of others—all of these should reflect the difference Jesus has made in our lives. We're to be different. An example to others who don't know Christ. We are "Exhibit A" as to what a Christian is all about.

Don't let anyone look down on you because you are young, but set an example for the believers in speech, in conduct, in love, in faith and in purity. (1 Tim. 4:12)

Summing It Up

Quarters made after 1964 aren't real silver—and neither are Susan B. Anthony dollars. They're just made to look like the real deal at a glance. Now take a look at the grooved edge of a quarter and a Susan B. Notice that at the center of the coins, the very heart of them is copper-colored? That's because it is copper. On the outside the coins appear to be silver, but at the very heart of both coins, they don't even pretend to be. This is the issue with Susan B. Anthony Christians. They have a heart problem. At their very core—at the very center of some Christians—we find compromise. Not a sold-out, fully dedicated desire to follow Jesus but only a desire to look that way.

Now look at the old Peace dollar. It is really silver all the way through—even at the heart of the coin. Sometimes we need to examine ourselves. Where are our hearts? Do we truly want to live for Jesus, or do we just want to look that way?

As Christians, we are dollar coins . . . children of the King. We hold so much value because of what Jesus did for us. But we have decisions to make. We can live like the world, with behavior and choices that aren't much different from those of people who don't know Jesus. Or we can live with grateful hearts, desiring to become more and more like Jesus. The choice is ours.

My hope is that you choose to be different—solid silver—so that people will know instantly that you are a follower of Jesus Christ.

As you end this, if you have a Susan B. Anthony dollar to give each of them, that would be great. Let it be a reminder that they want to be different from the world. And if you picked up a Peace dollar for each of them, this also is the time to give it to them. Explain that you hope every time they see it, they will be reminded to be a follower of Jesus right to their very core . . . right to their heart.

Practice Makes Perfect

THEME: Practice is needed to become good at almost anything, and that can apply to the Christian walk too.

THINGS YOU'LL NEED

- ☐ An instrument you don't really know how to play. This is something you'll likely borrow from a family member or a friend. You need a legit instrument here . . . a guitar, trombone, violin, or whatever. Sorry, a kazoo won't do. You'll want to select something that can't be played— and sound good—without a lot of practice.

Advance Prep

Nothing needed except lining up that instrument to borrow. And if you can borrow some sheet music at the same time, terrific.

Running the Activity

Get the kids together, pull out the instrument, and tell them you're going to play them the song on the sheet music—or a song they'd all know. Tell them the title of the song you're going to play. "Twinkle, Twinkle, Little Star" makes a nice choice. Now, the notes you play should sound nothing like the real song. The worse you are, the better you'll be able to illustrate the truth of this lesson.

If you'd rather have one of the kids play the instrument, that can work too. Obviously, you just need to be really careful if the instrument is borrowed.

Teaching the Lesson

Okay, if you were to rank from one to ten how well I played that song, what kind of score would you give me?

To be good at playing an instrument, it takes something more than just having a good instrument, right? And it takes more than just having sheet music with the notes on there too.

What is it you need to do if you're going to get good at playing any kind of instrument or any sport, or to be good at driving, drama, art, or something else?

We all know that to get good at something, likely we need to practice. These kinds of skills don't just come naturally. They don't come without us deliberately aiming at a goal and working toward it.

In some ways, the Christian life is the same. Think about what the Bible tells us we should be doing:

- Loving others
- Forgiving others
- Being kind
- Not sinning when we get angry

- Not being selfish
- Running from temptation
- Being a good example of believers
- Learning to trust God more

These things don't always come naturally, do they? We could add plenty more to that list too. But if we want to be better at these things, certainly we can ask God to help us—and he will. The Bible also makes it really clear that we're to *practice* doing the right things. That's the point of this example Jesus gave.

> Therefore everyone who hears these words of mine and **puts them into practice** is like a wise man who built his house on the rock. The rain came down, the streams rose, and the winds blew and beat against that house; yet it did not fall, because it had its foundation on the rock. But everyone who hears these words of mine and **does not put them into practice** is like a foolish man who built his house on sand. The rain came down, the streams rose, and the winds blew and beat against that house, and it fell with a great crash. (Matt. 7:24–27, emphasis added)

It's not enough to simply know what the Bible says. We have to put it into practice. Jesus says the person who does that is wise. By building good habits, when the storms of life come, we'll be in the habit of doing the right thing.

The person who knows what the Bible says but *doesn't* practice doing those things is acting foolishly. There will be times coming when they'll desperately need to do the things the Bible says—but since they haven't developed the habit of doing those things, they won't be able to do them in the moments they need to most. Since they haven't put those things into practice, they'll be unprepared. They will lose out in huge ways.

The unprepared person in the story Jesus told lost everything.

Summing It Up

Having an instrument in my hands doesn't make me a skilled musician. And holding a Bible in my hands—or even reading it—doesn't make me skilled at living the Christian life either. Can you imagine a musician only reading the music—and not actually playing the notes with the instrument? They could read music all day but probably wouldn't be able to play the instrument any better than before they started reading.

In the same way, we need to put the commands and principles we learn from the Bible into practice. We have to work at it a bit. And as we do, we'll get better and better at applying God's Word. We'll be in the habit of doing the right things. God will help us do that if we ask him.

Our people must learn to devote themselves to doing what is good . . . and not live unproductive lives. (Titus 3:14)

Micro Mess

THEME: The danger of hiding sin in our lives instead of dealing with it.

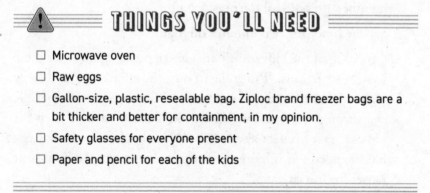

THINGS YOU'LL NEED

- ☐ Microwave oven
- ☐ Raw eggs
- ☐ Gallon-size, plastic, resealable bag. Ziploc brand freezer bags are a bit thicker and better for containment, in my opinion.
- ☐ Safety glasses for everyone present
- ☐ Paper and pencil for each of the kids

Advance Prep

You'll want to test this in advance. Every microwave is a little different, and eggs can be a bit unpredictable. You don't want the kids watching while you blow up an egg in the microwave oven for the first time. Testing this in advance is all about knowing what to expect when you do this live—and it allows you to stay more focused on the kids as a result.

So, test this out when they aren't around, and you'll likely do that much better of a job when you're with the kids.

Running the Activity

Be sure everyone present is wearing safety glasses or goggles—including you.

1. Cut one corner off the clear plastic bag. The reason? You don't want the bag to seal . . . not even by accident. It simply makes too big of a combustion chamber.

2. Slip the raw egg in the bag and put the bag in the microwave oven with the egg dead center on the little revolving plate. Remember, do not seal the plastic bag.

3. Set the timer for two minutes on high.

4. Give each of the kids some paper and a pencil, going over these basic instructions. "I'm going to start the microwave, and every eight or ten seconds I'll say 'time.' I want you to look at the egg through the window." (Not too close . . . always keep the kids at least five feet away.) "You're looking to see if that egg has changed—if it has gotten bigger. If not, jot 'NC' on your paper for 'no change.'"

Everybody still have safety glasses on? Is everyone at least five feet away? You may want to dim the lights a bit to make it easier to see inside the microwave. Okay . . . now start the microwave. Eight seconds later, call "time" and let them take a quick look—still from five feet away. "Do you see any change to the size of the egg . . . is that egg getting bigger? If not, jot NC on the paper."

Repeat that procedure until the egg blows up. Usually that will be within a minute or less.

Once the egg has exploded, open the microwave door and pick up the plastic bag by a top corner. It will be hot, so be careful or wear gloves.

Show the kids the plastic bag with the egg shrapnel inside. Steam will be pouring out the top.

Now look at their notes. You should see a series of NC, NC, NC—and then, sometime after that, the egg exploded. Ask them this question: "I see no change, no change, no change on your notes. Was there really no change and then this egg suddenly exploded?"

The kids all likely know that this wasn't random at all. There was no visible change on the outside, but the microwave was cooking the egg on the *inside*. That's how a microwave works.

Great job! You're ready to teach a really important lesson to the kids.

KEEP IT SAFE

If the timer goes over a minute and the egg hasn't exploded yet, back the kids away and turn off the microwave. I never let the egg go past seventy-five seconds. Likely there is a micro crack in the egg, and it is letting pressure out. Or maybe you're going to get a really big boom—which may not be the best idea. Wait at least two minutes for the egg to cool before you open the door. Toss the egg in the garbage and try with a new egg.

Teaching the Lesson

This egg in the microwave activity is a picture of life. We all probably had a good idea that a raw egg didn't belong in the microwave. And sometimes we as Christians can allow wrong things in our lives too. Some sort of sin. It could be pride. Unforgiveness. Jealousy. Dishonesty. Greed. Hypocrisy. Anger. Selfishness. Anything that we know is wrong . . . but instead of dealing with it—instead of getting it out of our lives—we hide it inside.

The thing is, we might think that the sin we hide inside isn't changing us. We can look in the mirror and see no change. We can sit at the kitchen table with Mom or Dad—and they don't seem to notice a change either. We can begin to believe there is no change happening to us. We can believe we can handle whatever it is we're hiding inside, without it having any effect on us.

But the thing we need to remember? Sin, deliberately hidden inside us, works like a microwave. It changes us on the inside. It changes our hearts.

And even if Mom and Dad don't realize what you're hiding in your life, who definitely *won't* miss it?

There is nothing concealed that will not be disclosed, or hidden that will not be made known. What you have said in the dark will be heard in the daylight, and what you have whispered in the ear in the inner rooms will be proclaimed from the roofs. (Luke 12:2–3)

Nothing in all creation is hidden from God's sight. Everything is uncovered and laid bare before the eyes of him to whom we must give account. (Heb. 4:13)

Summing It Up

The thing is, you could fool Mom and Dad . . . for a time, anyway. It would break our hearts, but you could do it. But you can never fool God.

And you can't get past the "spiritual physics" of sin. If we choose to hide sin in our lives, it works like a raw egg in a microwave. Our sin will come out . . . and when it does, it makes a big mess.

Kids, if there is something in your life that doesn't belong there, you need to deal with it before that sin makes a terrible mess. We can help with that. Talk to us. But don't do what the Pharisees did in the New Testament, where they pretended to be much better than they really were. They tried to hide their sin, but they couldn't hide it from Jesus. Hiding sin—instead of dealing with it—never ends well. Instead, let's confess our sins. Get rid of their weight. As we do, we'll be much more effective in whatever God has planned for us.

Therefore, since we are surrounded by such a great cloud of witnesses, let us throw off everything that hinders and the sin that so easily entangles. And let us run with perseverance the race marked out for us, fixing our eyes on Jesus, the pioneer and perfecter of faith. (Heb. 12:1–2)

Green Eggs and Ham Scam

THEME: The danger of envy and jealousy.

THINGS YOU'LL NEED

☐ Green liquid food coloring

☐ A meal made up of things that will absorb the green food coloring well. Remember, a little food coloring goes a long way. Rice, mashed potatoes, and cream-based sauces all absorb the green well. We chose scrambled eggs with French toast. You can even mix green coloring in the milk and in the butter for the toast. Or, if you want to tie into the classic Dr. Seuss book, *Green Eggs and Ham*, substitute ham for the French toast.

☐ *Green Eggs and Ham* by Dr. Seuss. Available at the library—or from friends with kids in the right age range. Just ask around.

Advance Prep

You may want to test making different foods with the green coloring so you have a feel for how much to use.

Running the Activity

Serve your green meal to the family. When they ask why you've added the coloring, you might mention that you wanted to make a point. While the meal may not look appetizing, it's harmless to eat. But explain that after you're done eating, you'll talk about something else we often refer to as "green." The difference is, if this green thing gets inside us, it can be really, really dangerous . . . even deadly.

Teaching the Lesson

Envy . . . or jealousy. Sometimes it's referred to as the "green monster," and for good reason. There are plenty of characters in the Bible who hurt themselves and others because of envy or jealousy.

- Cain: envious of Abel's offering being accepted by God (Gen. 4:3–5).
- Saul: jealous of David's popularity with the people (1 Sam. 18:5–9).
- Sarai: envious of her servant Hagar's ability to have children (Gen. 16:1–6).
- Martha: jealous of her sister Mary spending her time with Jesus (Luke 10:38–42).
- The Pharisees: jealous of Jesus's power and his popularity with the people (Matt. 27:18).

As a result, here's some of the things that happened.

- Cain killed his brother.
- Saul tried to kill David, alienated his own family, weakened his kingdom, and undermined his own authority.
- Sarai had her husband kick Hagar out along with her son, which began a conflict that still rages between nations.
- Martha complained to Jesus, but he corrected Martha, showing she was wrong. That had to be embarrassing to Martha.
- Many of the Pharisees missed their chance to follow Jesus—and kept others from following him too. Tragic, don't you think?

Bad things come into our lives, hurting us and others, when we allow envy or jealousy a foothold. Take a look at some of the things the Bible has to say about envy and jealousy.

> A heart at peace gives life to the body,
>> but envy rots the bones. (Prov. 14:30)

> Do not fret because of evildoers
>> or be envious of the wicked,
> for the evildoer has no future hope,
>> and the lamp of the wicked will be snuffed out. (24:19–20)

> Anger is cruel and fury overwhelming,
>> but who can stand before jealousy? (27:4)

For where you have envy and selfish ambition, there you find disorder and every evil practice. (James 3:16)

Do you see how dangerous envy and jealousy are?

Summing It Up

In the *Green Eggs and Ham* children's book, the character resists eating the meal every time it is offered to him. Eventually he tries it and finds out he can handle it after all. He's okay with green eggs and ham after that. That's fine for a story about green eggs, but we never want to relax our guard and allow envy or jealousy a place in our lives. We don't want to fall for the devil's "green eggs and ham scam" and start to think a little bit of jealousy is as harmless as green food coloring.

People get envious about all kinds of things:

- Somebody else's looks, smarts, abilities, popularity, or parents.
- Somebody else's family, friends, finances, or boyfriend/girlfriend.
- Somebody else's bike, car, phone, game system, or anything else they own.

If envy or jealousy take root in us, they become destructive and generally lead to sin. We can become mean. Bitter. Vindictive. All of that is pretty ugly stuff, isn't it? So let me encourage you . . . when you see that green monster show up in your life, ask God to help you get rid of it right away, before it hurts you—and those who love you.

The Missing Ingredient

THEME: The need to love others.

THINGS YOU'LL NEED

☐ Chocolate chip cookie recipe and all the tools and ingredients for making them. If you don't have a recipe, check online or use the recipe printed on the back of the chocolate chip bag. *Note: We will be modifying the recipe by reducing the amount of sugar we put in the dough— which will drastically change the taste.*

Advance Prep

Make the cookies in advance, and get as many of the kids involved as you can.

You'll want any kids present to help as you're mixing the ingredients. When it comes to the part about adding the granulated (white) sugar and the brown sugar, you're going to modify the recipe—and you'll want the kids to be aware of it. Say something like, "I want to try the cookies without so much sugar this time. So, we'll skip the white sugar completely and only use a quarter cup of the brown sugar instead of a three-quarter cup." (Note: this amount is based on a single batch, using the Nestlé Toll House Semi-Sweet Morsels recipe.)

Now, here's the toughest part of the advance prep. You don't want any of the kids sampling the cookie dough or the freshly baked cookies. They won't taste right with so little sugar, and you don't want the kids to experience that until you're teaching the lesson.

Running the Activity

Have the cookies on a plate and bring them out as you gather for family devotions. Invite them to enjoy the cookies while you talk: "I've modified the recipe by leaving out most of the sugar. I'd really like your input on how you like them. So, on a scale of one to ten, one being terrible and ten being I should open a business and start selling these, where would you rank this batch of cookies?"

Likely you'll get a pretty low ranking. Perfect.

Teaching the Lesson

So, you didn't like these, even though we baked these at the right temperature and for the right amount of time? And even though the flour and eggs and chocolate chips are all there . . . everything but the sugar . . . that one change to the recipe made *that* much difference?

I did this for a reason, to show you how life can be like a batch of chocolate chip cookies. There are specific "ingredients," or character qualities, that each of us should have. The Bible tells us that these things should be present in our lives as followers of Christ.

We're going to look at one of those ingredients today. And if that one thing is missing, we may look okay, but we're not going to be very appetizing to others. Anybody want to guess what that character quality is?

Listen to these Bible verses.

If I speak in the tongues of men or of angels, but do not have love, I am only a resounding gong or a clanging cymbal. If I have the gift of prophecy and can fathom all mysteries and all knowledge, and if I have a faith that can move mountains, but do not have love, I am nothing. If I give all I possess to the poor and give over my body to hardship that I may boast, but do not have love, I gain nothing. (1 Cor. 13:1–3)

That ingredient—that essential character quality that we need in our lives—is love.

When I left the sugar out of the chocolate chip cookies, I was wasting my time. The cookies didn't turn out right, even though they may have looked okay. You didn't enjoy their taste. Which means I'll probably end up tossing these out.

And as followers of Christ, we can have all kinds of great things in our lives, but if we're missing love, we won't turn out how God intended us to, and we won't exactly be appetizing to others.

So many times we are so deliberate about putting good things in our life. Good ingredients—like a great education, or developing great skills and abilities. We can do good things. But according to God's Word, if we leave love out of the mix, we're wasting our time. If we're living this Christian life—and not working at loving others? We're not following God's recipe for the Christian life at all.

When we talk about loving others, we're not talking about some kind of romantic, mushy thing. Loving others has to do with the next verses we see in that passage we just read.

Love is patient, love is kind. It does not envy, it does not boast, it is not proud. It does not dishonor others, it is not self-seeking, it is not easily angered, it keeps no record of wrongs. Love does not delight in evil but rejoices with the truth. It always protects, always trusts, always hopes, always perseveres.

Love never fails. (vv. 4–8)

Loving others has to do with being patient with them. Kind to them. Not being envious of them, and not bragging about ourselves when we're with them. Loving others means not putting them down—and doing what is best for them instead of just what we want to do. Loving others means we don't get angry with them very easily, and we don't hold grudges. Loving others means we protect them, and we build bridges of trust with them. We build hope. We don't give up or quit on someone. When we define love like that, can we begin to realize how essential it is to the Christian life?

Summing It Up

Can you see how loving others is as important in the life of a follower of Christ as sugar is to chocolate chip cookies? God wants us to be the type of person who attracts others so that they'll want to become disciples of Jesus too. But without love, we'll be the kind of person others avoid.

The sugar won't add itself to the cookies—and we tasted what happens when we ignore that part of the recipe. And in the Christian life, love doesn't just naturally show up either. Many times we need to add it in. It's something we deliberately work at. If we are followers of Christ, we have the Holy Spirit to help us. And remember, we can ask the Holy Spirit to help us love others the way we should. One of the fruits of the Spirit is love, right? Just like a tree produces fruit, the Holy Spirit can produce good fruit in our lives—like love.

> But the fruit of the Spirit is love, joy, peace, forbearance, kindness, goodness, faithfulness, gentleness and self-control. (Gal. 5:22–23)

If you want to make good cookies, don't forget the sugar. And if you want a life that is pleasing to God and others . . . don't forget the love. Love makes life better for you—and everyone around you. Love is the sugar of life!

> Love must be sincere. Hate what is evil; cling to what is good. Be devoted to one another in love. Honor one another above yourselves. (Rom. 12:9–10)

> Don't let anyone look down on you because you are young, but set an example for the believers in speech, in conduct, in love, in faith and in purity. (1 Tim. 4:12)

The Devil's Trap

THEME: Trusting God's plan for sex . . . and the danger of shortcutting that with pornography or premarital sex.

THINGS YOU'LL NEED

- ☐ Rat trap—available at a hardware store. The traditional kind that looks like a giant mouse trap. Wood base. Visible bait tab. Nasty, spring-loaded kill bar.
- ☐ Fine-point permanent marker
- ☐ White paint or white primer. You won't need much, so anything you have on hand will work. If you need to buy something, you can pick up a small plastic 2-ounce container of acrylic white paint at a hobby/craft store for cheap.
- ☐ Small paint brush to paint the rat trap

Advance Prep

We'll be talking about pornography and sex before marriage a bit today, so you'll want to be sure this is age appropriate for your kids. But before you skip this one, remember, your kids need to hear about this—and more than once. And chances are, they need to hear about this a lot younger than you'd like. So, read this over. Pray about it. Kids are getting exposed to porn and opportunities for sex at really young ages—and you don't want them unprepared. We have an enemy out there scheming to trap our kids in all kinds of ways that will hurt them, and today's lesson is about a big one.

Are you thinking you're not qualified to teach this? I've heard that from many, many parents. Maybe you failed in this very area when you were younger. If so, then you know how badly it can hurt people, and you definitely want to warn your kids. Don't let the enemy use guilt or shame to dupe you into leaving your kids unprotected. Remember, you've confessed those sins long ago, right? God chooses not to remember the sins he's forgiven, and that means his kids shouldn't remember their past sins and failures either.

Remember, no matter what your past was, your job *now* is to protect your kids . . . and that means from the traps of porn and premarital sex too. Okay, now that we have that settled, let's get at it.

We're not going to get into a whole lesson about why sex before marriage is wrong or why porn is wrong. That's too much to handle in one devotional. We just want to show the kids how these things

For more devotionals about premarital sex or porn, see devotional 29, Some Things ARE Black-and-White, in this book, volume 3. Also check out House of the Dead in volume 1 of *The Very Best, Hands-On, Kinda Dangerous Family Devotions* and Porn: Toxic. Twisting. Trap. in volume 2.

are used as bait—and the lies the devil tries to get us to believe so we don't see the trap.

Paint the wood base of the rat trap with the white paint. Likely some of the graphics from the manufacturer will still bleed through. That's perfect. You want that.

After the paint dries, write these words and phrases randomly on that wood base with your fine-point permanent marker.

- Satisfaction guaranteed!
- Safe!
- Feels great!
- You can handle this!
- You'll be glad you did!
- Thrilling and exciting!
- Nobody will know!
- No bad side effects!
- You'll be missing something if you don't!

Finally, take a small piece of paper or sticky note and write "Sex before marriage and pornography" on it. You'll stick or tape that on the little bait pad of the rat trap during the devotional, but just keep it on the side for now.

Running the Activity

Gather the kids around your rat trap. Say something like, "I have a rat trap here. I've painted over the thing, but you can still tell it's a trap, right?"

You'll definitely want them to get a feel for how powerful the trap is. You can do that in one of a few ways. While holding the trap in one hand (be careful that your fingers aren't in the way), pull back on the kill bar and let the spring snap it back in place. It should make a nice loud bang. Even better, actually set the trap. Do this on the floor or table, then use something like a broomstick to tap the bait pad to trigger the trap.

Or, if you really want to make an impression, use a fresh pencil to trigger the trap (and get out the safety glasses). The pencil should be long—nearly brand-new. Hold the pencil firmly, then press down hard on the bait pad. The kill bar should snap the pencil in two.

Once you've demonstrated the power of the trap, you can move on to teaching the lesson.

Teaching the Lesson

God created fire to do good things for us. Can you name any? (Keeps us warm. We can use it to cook. It gives us light. We can use it to purify things. It can keep us safe by scaring animals away.)

But fire, if not used properly, can do great damage too. A child playing with matches can cause a fire that can burn down a home or forest. Fire, used by someone in bad or wrong ways, can kill. It can scar.

So, God creates good things, but the devil often twists those things into something sinful. The devil and his demons often urge us to take things God created for good—and use them in wrong ways. Like our words. God created our mouths to say good, encouraging things to people, but our words can also be used to hurt us—and other people . . . to tear them down.

KEEP IT SAFE

You'll need safety glasses for you and the kids if you choose the pencil option for demonstrating the power of the trap.

Sex is another example. God created it to be a good thing, reserved exclusively for marriage. It can create wonderful kids, and it can strengthen a marriage in many ways. But the devil uses our desire for sex as bait to lure us into a trap. (*Get out your sticky note and place it on the bait pad of the trap.*)

The enemy uses sexual desire and pornography as bait and tries to keep us focused on the bait—and not the trap. In fact, there are some lies he uses to hide the trap. Let's take a look at some of these lies—and remind ourselves of the truth.

Satisfaction guaranteed! Actually, sex before marriage and viewing porn can lead to terrible regrets.

Safe! There is no such thing as safe sex. A condom may help prevent some disease or pregnancies, but manufacturers are really careful not to guarantee those. Sperm can penetrate a condom—resulting in pregnancy. Having sex with someone who has a disease that they aren't aware of can be absolutely deadly. And in the case of porn, watching the images rewires the brain in scary, scary ways. There are tons of reports and studies on this.

Feels great! True, but God designed sex for marriage. Period. Before marriage, sex can lead to great emotional pain—especially when you've given all to someone who breaks up with you later. And porn often leaves viewers feeling lousy about themselves.

You can handle this! Actually, you can't. Sex before marriage—and porn—are too powerful. They will impact you, and not in good ways. Pornography is absolutely and undeniably addicting—and it happens quick. It's a brain chemical thing, which is terrifying when you think about it.

You'll be glad you did! Often, taking the bait in one of these areas fills a person with guilt.

Thrilling and exciting! True, but the feeling doesn't last long. It leaves a person empty and, like a drug addict, searching for a way to get more.

Nobody will know! Wrong. God will know . . . and hidden sin tends to come out.

No bad side effects! Not true. Some damage may not show immediately—like the bad effects of rewiring the brain with porn. Actual physical sex can lead to disease, pregnancy, and all kinds of emotional complications.

You'll be missing something if you don't! True. You'll miss a lot of pain. Regret. Guilt. Emotional trauma. Brain rewiring. Potential for disease. And you'll be missing all the complications later, when you get married, that result from disregarding God's plan for sex.

Let's take a look at some verses from the Bible.

Flee from sexual immorality. All other sins a person commits are outside the body, but whoever sins sexually, sins against their own body. Do you not know that your bodies are temples of the Holy Spirit, who is in you, whom you have received from God? You are not your own; you were bought at a price. Therefore honor God with your bodies. (1 Cor. 6:18–20)

Flee the evil desires of youth and pursue righteousness, faith, love and peace, along with those who call on the Lord out of a pure heart. (2 Tim. 2:22)

Summing It Up

The devil will try convincing you to take God's good gift of sex—which God designed solely for marriage—and use it now. Sex before marriage and pornography are a couple of his most effective traps. Don't fall for them.

As followers of Jesus, we say we love him, don't we? We claim to love God. That's good. And let's remember what love does.

Love does not delight in evil but rejoices with the truth. It always protects, always trusts, always hopes, always perseveres. (1 Cor. 13:6–7)

And if we truly love God . . . remember how God defines love for him: *obedience*. If we don't obey God, we can't say we truly love him. We're only fooling ourselves.

Jesus replied, "Anyone who loves me will obey my teaching. My Father will love them, and we will come to them and make our home with them. Anyone who does not love me will not obey my teaching. These words you hear are not my own; they belong to the Father who sent me." (John 14:23–24)

Trust God enough to do life God's way . . . according to his plan for us. Trust him enough to wait for sex until marriage. God invented sex, and he knows how it will work best and most powerfully. Trust him. Wait.

A Special Word for Parents

Plan to create some one-on-one time with each of the kids—especially if they are older. See if the enemy already has them caught in the trap of porn, and show them how to break free. If you can get a copy of *Super Husband, Super Dad* by Tim Shoemaker, check out chapter 13 for some very real helps for breaking free.

One other thought. When talking to your kids about following God's plan to abstain from sex until marriage, realize that their definition of sex may be different from yours. For example, we would consider oral sex to be sex—but sometimes our culture teaches otherwise. You'll want to help the kids understand that when you talk about saving sex for marriage, you are talking about sex in all its forms.

And stay away from viewing other people in a sexual way—which is what pornography is all about. Sex, in all its forms, is created for marriage and is not to be part of our lives outside of marriage.

Mom and Dad hope that you see these things as they really are: traps. And it is our prayer that you avoid the devil's traps and all the hurt that comes with them.

Gagging Your Bragging

THEME: Genuine love doesn't brag. That's wrong—and kind of ugly.

THINGS YOU'LL NEED

☐ Photocopy of the skit printed at the end of this lesson

Advance Prep

You may want to take a look at the script you'll use for role-playing. If you want to change genders or names of the characters to make it relate to your family more, this is the time to do that.

Running the Activity

The skit at the end of this lesson is designed to be role-played by two people. Stephen, the new neighbor, is the braggart. You'll want to consider your family when you assign parts. Maybe you'll take the braggart role and let one of the kids be the nice neighbor. And depending on who you're giving the other role to, consider their personality. If they'd want the script in advance to read it through once or twice, that's fine. You want them to have fun during the devotional, and if previewing the script will help, let them do that.

If nobody in your family would be up for role-playing, you can simply read both parts yourself. Once the role-playing is done, move on to the lesson.

Teaching the Lesson

Okay, so the bragging was a little exaggerated in this script, but I think it makes the point. Bragging isn't very appealing, is it? It can be downright ugly.

God doesn't like bragging either. Why do you imagine he feels that way?

If I'm bragging, who does it put the spotlight on?

If I'm bragging, how might I be taking credit for something that would have been impossible without God?

If I'm bragging about how well I did in some way, who gave me that ability, that opportunity, that intelligence, and life itself?

When we think of it that way, God really deserves the credit for even the good things we do. When we take all the credit, isn't that a little like stealing from God?

The Bible has some pretty clear things to say about bragging.

Do nothing out of selfish ambition or vain conceit. Rather, in humility value others above yourselves, not looking to your own interests but each of you to the interests of the others. (Phil. 2:3–4)

This is what the LORD says:

> "Let not the wise boast of their wisdom
>   or the strong boast of their strength
>   or the rich boast of their riches,
> but let the one who boasts boast about this:
>   that they have the understanding to know me,
> that I am the LORD, who exercises kindness,
>   justice and righteousness on earth,
>   for in these I delight,"
>   declares the LORD. (Jer. 9:23–24)

Ultimately, without Christ, we are dead in our sins. Doomed to eternity in hell. Without any hope to save ourselves. By God's great grace, Jesus takes care of all those things. He does it all. We have nothing to brag about; we owe all our praise to him.

> For it is by grace you have been saved, through faith—and this is not from yourselves, it is the gift of God—not by works, so that no one can boast. (Eph. 2:8–9)

> It is because of him that you are in Christ Jesus, who has become for us wisdom from God—that is, our righteousness, holiness and redemption. Therefore, as it is written: "Let the one who boasts boast in the Lord." (1 Cor. 1:30–31)

That's why the apostle Paul wrote this:

> May I never boast except in the cross of our Lord Jesus Christ, through which the world has been crucified to me, and I to the world. (Gal. 6:14)

Summing It Up

Remember the story of David and Goliath in 1 Samuel 17?

Goliath bragged about himself. It was all about what he was going to do to David. How he was going to beat him, rip him apart, and feed him to the wild animals.

David bragged too. He bragged to King Saul about how he'd fought a wild bear and a lion when they tried to get away with sheep David was shepherding. He convinced the king to let him fight Goliath by explaining that *God* had rescued David from those wild animals. David fully believed that God would rescue him from Goliath too. David wasn't bragging about *himself*. He was bragging on God.

David bragged to Goliath too. But David bragged about the God he served. How God would deliver Goliath to him. David said that he'd kill Goliath and cut his head off—so that all would know that the all-powerful God of Israel did that.

David wasn't bragging about himself but about God. Do you see the difference between how Goliath bragged and how David did? Often, boasting or bragging is a way to put ourselves on a platform, on a pedestal, when God is the only one who belongs there. Bragging is an attempt to get people to admire us, praise us, and even, in a small way, worship us. No wonder God hates bragging. Praise and worship are things that belong only to God. He is in control and deserves all the credit. We can't even control tomorrow, can we? We can make plans, but we can't be sure it will work out the way we want. Only God can do that.

> Do not boast about tomorrow,
>> for you do not know what a day may bring. (Prov. 27:1)

It can be really easy to brag—especially when something really good happens. Let's remember how ugly bragging can be and how wrong it really is. Let's remember who really deserves the credit.

When we're tempted to brag, how can we turn that around so that we're bragging on God?

Gagging Your Bragging Skit

"The New Neighbor"

Cast of Characters

MEG: Girl living next door to the new neighbor. She has lived in the area all her life.

STEPHEN: The new, proud neighbor.

Setting

The scene is set at the front door of a new neighbor's home. As the scene opens, MEG walks up and rings the doorbell.

Scene

STEPHEN: (Opening door) Hi.

MEG: (Smiling) Hi, I'm Meg, your next-door neighbor. I saw the moving truck this morning and thought I'd stop by to welcome you to the neighborhood. You have a beautiful new home.

STEPHEN: (Looking doubtful) This place? This is a dump compared to where I used to live. Our last house had a pool. A four-car garage. It was way bigger.

MEG: It still looks nice to me.

STEPHEN: Because you haven't seen how dinky the closet is in my room. I can't even unpack all the boxes of my clothes. There's no room to hang them. And where to put all my trophies . . . that's the big problem.

MEG: Trophies?

STEPHEN: Tons of them. I'm a natural athlete—and not just in one sport. I haven't found a sport yet that I don't excel in. I'll probably be in the Olympics someday—coming home with a bazillion gold medals. The coach at my last school was really sorry we moved. The team doesn't have a chance at the championship without me.

MEG: (A little sarcastically) Wow . . . I guess I'm pretty lucky to have a star athlete like you living right next door.

STEPHEN: For sure. Your girlfriends at school will think you're the luckiest girl around. They'll want to come to your house all the time.

MEG: Just so they can be closer to you?

STEPHEN: (Grins and nods) What can I say? I'm kind of a big deal. Like a celebrity, you know? That's what happens when you're smart, athletic, and handsome like me. Oh yeah, the girls will come running.

MEG: (She's definitely heard enough bragging.) Which is exactly why I need to get going. If any of my friends see me here talking to you, they'll get so jealous that they won't speak to me for days.

STEPHEN: I can seriously see that happening.

MEG: (Backs away.)

STEPHEN: (Calling after her) I can't remember your name, but why don't you come by tomorrow—and bring some of your friends. By then I'll have unpacked my trophies. I can tell you all about how I won each of them—and I'll even let you take pictures of me with the trophies—for free. How's that sound?

MEG: Like way too much.

STEPHEN: (Smiling proudly) It's true. I'm probably the most generous guy you know.

Cut It Out!

THEME: Sometimes God prunes things out of our lives to make us more productive for his purposes.

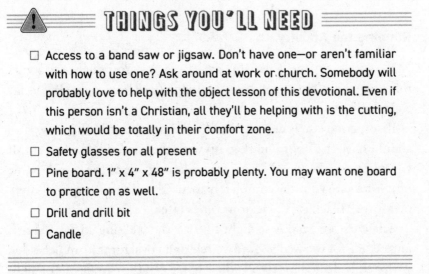

THINGS YOU'LL NEED

- [ ] Access to a band saw or jigsaw. Don't have one—or aren't familiar with how to use one? Ask around at work or church. Somebody will probably love to help with the object lesson of this devotional. Even if this person isn't a Christian, all they'll be helping with is the cutting, which would be totally in their comfort zone.
- [ ] Safety glasses for all present
- [ ] Pine board. 1" x 4" x 48" is probably plenty. You may want one board to practice on as well.
- [ ] Drill and drill bit
- [ ] Candle

Advance Prep

If you're talking to a friend/neighbor/coworker about using their saw . . . and they're willing to do the cutting? Terrific. Go with it. If you're borrowing a saw, be sure you've practiced cutting with it in advance.

Plan to cut out one or all of these shapes for the actual devotional. Pencil the lines in advance so you've got something to follow when the kids are present.

- **Door wedge.** Basically, a small wedge you might use to prop open a door.
- **Walking stick.** Could be just a 1.5″ cut running the entire length of the board. If you want to get fancy, you can add a curved top to make a cane.
- **Candleholder.** You might cut out a circle with a hole drilled dead center to hold a candle. You'll need a bit that's the right diameter to hold the candle snuggly. Be sure to test it on a piece of scrap wood in advance.

Running the Activity

Make sure everyone is wearing safety glasses. You might say something like this. "We've got a nice-looking board here, right? But today we're going to cut it up."

If someone else is cutting the wood, have them do that now. You should have the board marked up with the shapes you want cut. If you're cutting the wood—or if you're letting one of the kids do some of it—be sure you stay completely focused on the cutting and safety measures. Teaching the lesson comes later.

The cuts are easy. A straight line for the walking stick. A short, angled line for the wedge. And a circle or an oval for the candleholder, with a hole drilled for the candle itself. Keep the candle out of sight until you complete the candleholder.

As the cuts are being made, scraps and sawdust are dropping. Great. You'll refer to that later. Once all the pieces are finished—and the hole is drilled to fit the candle—you're ready to move on. If you'll be teaching the lesson from a different location, bag up the big chunks of scrap that dropped to the floor and bring them with you.

Teaching the Lesson

We started out with a really nice piece of wood, then cut a lot of good wood away to come up with these three shapes—and a whole lot of scraps.

Did it seem like we were wasting a perfectly nice board when we cut it up like that?

Sometimes life can feel a little bit like this. Let's imagine we're the board. Sometimes it feels like God is cutting things away from us, doesn't it? Maybe we lose a friend or loved one. Maybe we don't make the team. Maybe we have a lost opportunity, or we move away from friends and the house we call home. It could be a thousand things.

When perfectly good things get cut out of our lives, often it hurts. It may feel unfair. It may seem like God doesn't love us quite as much as we thought he did.

The reality is, often God cuts things from our lives *because* he loves us. It is about making us more productive. More fruitful.

I am the true vine, and my Father is the gardener. He cuts off every branch in me that bears no fruit, while every branch that does bear fruit he prunes so that it will be even more fruitful. (John 15:1–2)

God has plans for us . . . things he's prepared for us to do.

For we are God's handiwork, created in Christ Jesus to do good works, which God prepared in advance for us to do. (Eph. 2:10)

Often, we don't even know what those plans are. But *he* knows—and often he is shaping our lives so that we are better suited to do the very things he's created us to do.

Think about the things we cut out a few minutes ago.

- **Door wedge.** Maybe God is making you into a person who is really effective at opening doors of opportunity for others. A wedge is designed to do that efficiently, but a board would only be in the way.
- **Walking stick.** Maybe God has plans for you to help others in their walk with Christ. He may be turning you into a walking stick or a cane of sorts. One who others can lean on. Depend on. One who disciples others in their walk with the Lord. Maybe he's cutting away the things that don't belong in your life or that would distract from the real purpose he has for you. A board is nice, but it isn't very effective when it comes to helping someone walk. But a cane or a walking stick will do the job nicely.
- **Candleholder.** Maybe God wants you to shine for him in a special way—or wants you to lift him up so others see his light. Shaping you into a candleholder will make you a whole lot more effective at that than leaving you as a board.

Summing It Up

When God cuts things out of our lives, it generally isn't pleasant.

- He may be making us better suited to do the jobs he has for us.
- He may be cutting some things out so we become more compassionate toward others who are facing hardships.
- God may be refining our character. Making us more humble. More loving. More patient. Less angry.

- God may be cutting things from our lives that simply don't belong there. Pride. Selfishness. Unforgiveness.

Whatever the reasons God cuts things out of our lives, we can always be sure it is for our good and his glory.

And we know that in all things God works for the good of those who love him, who have been called according to his purpose. For those God foreknew he also predestined to be conformed to the image of his Son, that he might be the firstborn among many brothers and sisters. (Rom. 8:28–29)

So, when we feel God is cutting things away from us, let's work at not complaining about it. Let's trust that what God is doing is pruning us . . . trimming things away so that we're more productive and more able to accomplish his good purposes.

Tools of the Trade

Honesty versus lies and deception.

THINGS YOU'LL NEED

☐ Stories and headlines from a tabloid type newspaper. You'll want to clip out at least four, five, or hopefully more stories that are clearly bogus. The more bizarre the better. Not the celebrity gossip stories, but other stories that are just ridiculous—and obviously not true. Some of the content in those papers is inappropriate, so I wouldn't let the kids browse through it. Just clip the stories you want to use with the kids and toss the rest.

☐ You can find outlandish stories from online sources as well. When you find one that works for you and the family, print it out so you have a physical copy to show the kids. Another way to do this is to Google "outrageous tabloid headlines," and you'll get plenty of crazy examples. You won't even have to print out the full story. Printing the headlines alone will make it clear that the stories are not true.

Advance Prep

No advance prep needed other than gathering those stories and head-lines. I did a quick search online to find examples of tabloid headlines that would work well. Below is a sampling. And, of course, all of these came with photos—because we know that pictures don't lie, right?

- "Titanic Survivors Found Onboard"
- "Fish Has Human Face!"
- "Alien Super-Men Target Earth!"
- "Tragedy as Body of Hide-and-Seek World Champion Found in Cupboard"
- "Strange Breed of Cats Found on Mars!"
- "Missing Plane Found on the Moon!"

Running the Activity

Have fun with this! If reading level permits, give each of the kids a couple articles and/or headlines to look over. Tell them you'll give them a few minutes to skim, then each of them will share their stories/headlines with the others. Ultimately, they need to make a decision of whether or not they feel each story is entirely true.

Those kids whose reading level may not be up to the task can team up with an older sibling. If that isn't possible, Mom or Dad can just read the headlines and stories—then ask the obvious question.

This is intended to be a fun activity, not homework. If your kids aren't old enough to do the reading, then you can go over the articles and headlines with them. Just the headline or a quick synopsis of the story should give them enough information to make a decision as to whether the story is completely true or not. With each story/headline, ask the obvious question: "Do you think this story/headline is entirely true or not?"

Teaching the Lesson

Okay, obviously we can't believe everything we read. Why do you think people write such crazy stories? Do you think the owners of these kinds of newspapers are really interested in the truth, or in selling more newspapers?

In real life, there are lots of times people don't tell the truth—or they don't tell the whole truth. Why do you think people do that? Here are four reasons I can think of.

One, to avoid something uncomfortable or unpleasant. Sometimes people don't tell others the truth because they think they'll feel uncomfortable. If asked, "How did you like my solo in the play?" they say what they think the person asking the question wants to hear, rather than tell the truth in a nice way. "Oh, your solo in the musical was fantastic! Next time you should try for the lead role."

Two, to avoid punishment or consequences. Sometimes people mess up and do something that will likely get them in trouble. So, in order to avoid the deserved punishment, they lie about it—or don't tell the whole truth. "It wasn't me."

Three, to get something they wouldn't get with the truth. Sometimes people lie to get something they want from somebody else. Something they wouldn't get if the other person knew the truth. Maybe somebody wants to go out with friends—but Mom asks if their homework is finished. If they tell the truth, they won't be able to go, so they lie. "I don't have any homework."

Four, to protect themselves or somebody else. Maybe they saw somebody steal something out of a backpack. But when questioned about it, they say they didn't see anything in order to protect the thief—or themselves.

Some people think these are all good reasons to lie. But here's a couple of good reasons *not* to lie:

1. God hates lies.
2. God punishes liars.

Let's look at some verses from the Bible.

> There are six things the LORD hates,
>   seven that are detestable to him:
>   haughty eyes,
>   a lying tongue,
>   hands that shed innocent blood,
>   a heart that devises wicked schemes,
>   feet that are quick to rush into evil,
>   a false witness who pours out lies
>   and a person who stirs up conflict in the community.
>   (Prov. 6:16–19)

Did you notice that two of the seven things above have to do with dishonesty?

> A false witness will not go unpunished,
>   and whoever pours out lies will not go free. (19:5)

> Whoever of you loves life
>   and desires to see many good days,
> keep your tongue from evil
>   and your lips from telling lies.
> Turn from evil and do good;
>   seek peace and pursue it. (Ps. 34:12–14)

Summing It Up

Clearly, God isn't a fan of lies. Lies and deception are trademarks of the devil. They are tools of his trade.

You belong to your father, the devil, and you want to carry out your father's desires. He was a murderer from the beginning, not holding to the truth, for there is no truth in him. When he lies, he speaks his native language, for he is a liar and the father of lies. (John 8:44)

The devil is considered the father of lies, so when we lie, we are acting a whole lot more like the devil than our heavenly Father. That doesn't sound like a good thing at all.

Let me encourage you to dedicate yourself to telling the truth—all the time. Let's not settle for telling only part of the truth while leaving other parts out. Let's not settle for staying quiet when we should speak up. Sometimes our silence can be a form of lying too.

Let's dedicate ourselves to being honest all the time . . . even if it means we're going to get in big trouble. Let's be careful not to be like the father of lies but more like our heavenly Father instead.

Do not lie to each other, since you have taken off your old self with its practices and have put on the new self, which is being renewed in knowledge in the image of its Creator. (Col. 3:9–10)

New Lesson from an Old Game

THEME: Fighting selfishness and putting the needs of others first instead.

THINGS YOU'LL NEED

- [ ] Sturdy folding chairs—or any type of chair (preferably without arms). You'll want a chair for each person present for devotions.
- [ ] Phone with a music app. Something you can mute and unmute quickly. A TV remote works fine for this as well.
- [ ] Prize for the winner of the game. Give this some thought. You want to pick something your kids would like to win. But it doesn't mean you need to spend any money. Do you have them do chores weekly? Maybe you'll do the winner's chores this week. Or maybe the winner gets to stay up an extra half hour later than the others at bedtime. Get creative.

Advance Prep

No advance prep needed.

Running the Activity

Set the chairs up in a row, side by side. Alternate the direction of every other chair. Explain they're going to play a game of musical chairs. Back when their grandparents were kids, this was a standard birthday party game.

Go over the rules. The kids march around the row of chairs while the music plays. When the music stops, they need to scramble to find a chair to sit in. The person without a chair is out.

Do a practice run so everyone gets the feel of it. Now remove the first chair so there is one less chair than kids looking for a seat and start the music. Every time a person is out, you remove one more chair, start up the music, and do the little marching routine around the chairs all over again.

Repeat until you have only one chair and two kids left—and ultimately that one winner who will get the prize. *Note: If you notice any of the kids deliberately letting one of their siblings have the chair—just to be nice to them—you'll be able to use that later.*

Teaching the Lesson

When you're playing musical chairs, you're concentrating: listening for the music to stop, watching the empty chairs, and knowing which one you'll scramble for if the music stops at that moment. You don't want to be the one left without a chair. The game is all about doing what is best for yourselves, isn't it?

In life, that's the way some people act every day. They're focused on doing what is best for themselves. They may even push others out of their way, in a sense, to get what they want before someone else snags it. Have you seen others do things like that? For example, sometimes we see people drive like they own the road. They tailgate, honk their horn, weave in and out of lanes, and cut others off. They're all about doing what they think is best for themselves. They're all about getting what they want.

As followers of Christ, we're to do life differently from the way so many others do. We don't see Jesus pushing others or rushing to get ahead of them. He isn't out there looking to do what's best for himself. He's all about doing what God the Father wants him to do. We see no better example of this than when he prayed shortly before he was arrested.

> Going a little farther, he fell with his face to the ground and prayed, "My Father, if it is possible, may this cup be taken from me. Yet not as I will, but as you will." (Matt. 26:39)

And Jesus is all about doing what's best for other people.

> The thief comes only to steal and kill and destroy; I have come that they may have life, and have it to the full. (John 10:10)

Summing It Up

Looking out solely for ourselves is fine in a silly game like musical chairs. But in real life, as Christians, we're to imitate how Jesus treats others. He is our example, isn't he? We can't be so focused on ourselves that we don't consider what others may be feeling or thinking. We want to see others like Jesus does, and seek ways to put their interests and concerns ahead of ours.

Do nothing out of selfish ambition or vain conceit. Rather, in humility value others above yourselves, not looking to your own interests but each of you to the interests of the others. (Phil. 2:3–4)

Jesus wants us to work at putting others first . . . and that includes brothers or sisters. So many arguments, even here in our own family, would cease to exist if we really put these verses into practice, don't you think?

Is that always going to be easy? Not at all. But think of what Jesus has done. He left heaven—why? Because earth would be more comfortable for him? No. In fact, earth was clearly a much worse place to live, but he made that sacrifice so he could save people who needed rescuing, which includes us.

Let's ask God to help us put others first—including right here in our own family—even more often than we're doing now. In fact, let's each think of a way we can put someone else first today.

Sometimes we think that unless we look out for ourselves, we won't get ahead. But let's remember that when we put others first, God knows it. And he rewards those who follow the example Jesus gave us.

Now . . . it's time to reward the musical chairs winner.

During the game, did you observe any of the kids giving up their chair willingly—allowing someone else to get a seat? It would be good to tell them you noticed that. And to really reinforce the point of the lesson, give them a reward, too, by giving them a similar prize.

Follow That Car

THEME: Being a good example to others, even when we don't think others are watching.

THINGS YOU'LL NEED

☐ Your car. How's that for easy?

Advance Prep

No advance prep needed.

Running the Activity

Get the kids buckled into the car and explain what you'll be doing. Tell them, "I'm going to have one of you pick a car or truck, and we're going to follow it for a bit. If we get bored following that vehicle, we'll just choose a different one." When you follow them, you'll have two goals.

1. Don't lose sight of them.
2. Don't let them have any idea they're being followed.

Start by having one of the kids pick a vehicle to follow. You can have them do that as soon as you pull out onto the road, or you may wait until you drive to a high traffic area. If you have a street with fast-food restaurants nearby, that can be a great place to start.

Keep a safe distance from the car you're following—and definitely avoid tailgating. Are they speeding? You may want to mention that. But have all the kids involved in watching the car.

If the car pulls into a grocery store lot, pull in after them. Let the kids decide whether to wait for the driver to come out of the store and continue following them or to pick a new car.

If the car you're following pulls into a fast-food drive-thru lane, pull in right behind them. This would be pure gold and the ultimate

KEEP IT SAFE

If you're the driver, you'll want to really use your head here. When following, allow plenty of distance between you and the vehicle you're tracking. If you can have a car or two in between you, that will help hide the fact you're tailing them.

If, by some remote chance, the driver you're following starts driving erratically, or maybe they sense you're following and they speed up to lose you, do not chase them. That would be a really, really bad example to the kids—and would defeat the whole objective of the lesson. Just choose a new car to follow.

way for the kids to remember the point of this lesson. It may not happen, but if it does, don't hesitate to follow. When you get to the ordering speaker, just tell the person taking the order that you'd like exactly what the car ahead of you ordered. When you get the food, either take it inside to divvy it out or bring it home to see what you got. The kids will think you're either absolutely crazy or totally cool. Honestly, it's a total win either way—because they'll never forget this devotional.

Generally, ten minutes is plenty for the following game. You don't want the kids to get bored and lose interest. Now you'll transition to the spiritual truth that you want to get across. You can tie it in as you drive or, better yet, go back home or park the car somewhere so you can focus on them as you finish the lesson.

Teaching the Lesson

Do you think the other vehicle's driver had a clue that we were following them? That we were watching their every move?

This is a lot like life. There are people we follow. Imitate. They could be friends. They could be people we don't know—or hardly know at all. Sometimes we pick them because there's something we admire about them, or we want to be like them in some way. Or maybe we respect them, and so we tend to watch what they do . . . and how they react in situations. Sometimes that's fine, but following someone can be disastrous too. It all depends on who you're following and what they do. Let me encourage you to choose wisely who you follow. If we choose poorly, following them could change us in bad ways.

Do not be misled: "Bad company corrupts good character." (1 Cor. 15:33)

If someone we're following makes a bad decision, we need to break away and not make the same mistake.

> My son, if sinful men entice you,
>   do not give in to them. (Prov. 1:10)

Summing It Up

Let's take this one step further. Did you ever stop to think that some people may be following you? It could be a younger brother or sister, a cousin, or somebody from church or school. It may be someone that you'd never guess was following you—because they're careful not to make it obvious—just like I was when we followed that car.

So, here are some questions:

> If someone followed you when you weren't aware of it, would you lead them to a place that was good, or bad? Would following you lead them closer to God, or away?
>
> If someone younger than you did the same things you're doing, would they be in a better place, or might following you cause them to sin in some way?
>
> If someone talked the way you talked to others or adopted your attitudes, would they be a better person for it, or worse?

In the Bible, the apostle Paul was keenly aware people were watching him and following him. But that was okay, because he was careful to live in a way that wouldn't lead someone in a bad direction—even if he didn't realize anyone was following. Here's what he said in one of his letters:

> Whatever you have learned or received or heard from me, or seen in me—put it into practice. And the God of peace will be with you. (Phil. 4:9)

Others will likely follow us at different times in our lives—even if we don't know it. Even if we don't want them to. So, don't you think we need to be careful about how we live? There are some scary verses that talk about the danger we're in if we do things that cause others to sin.

Jesus said to his disciples: "Things that cause people to stumble are bound to come, but woe to anyone through whom they come. It would be better for them to be thrown into the sea with a millstone tied around their neck than to cause one of these little ones to stumble. So watch yourselves." (Luke 17:1–3)

Let's be careful who we follow. Ultimately, Jesus is our example, right?

Then he called the crowd to him along with his disciples and said: "Whoever wants to be my disciple must deny themselves and take up their cross and follow me." (Mark 8:34)

And it is my prayer that you remember to live in a way that is worth following too—even if you don't think anyone is watching.

Bashed Burritos

THEME: Our anger has a way of making a mess—and messing up others too.

THINGS YOU'LL NEED

- ☐ Baseball bat—wood or aluminum. A Wiffle ball bat won't have enough oomph.
- ☐ At least two or three burritos for each of your kids. You can make your own or go to a fast-food restaurant where you can get them cheap. I went to Taco Bell.
- ☐ Safety glasses for all present

Advance Prep

Be sure you've got a nice, wide-open space to do this. This devotional will make a mess. And you may want to think about what you—and the kids—are wearing. This may not be the day for wearing your Sunday best.

Now, it would really be good to test this in advance. It's best to sling a couple of rubber bands around each burrito so it won't fall apart when you pitch it to the batter. You could also wrap a piece of duct tape around it. See what works best for you.

Running the Activity

Take the kids in the car to pick up the burritos, or you may have already picked them up in advance. Now go to the place you've chosen to play burrito baseball.

Explain that you're going to pitch the burritos, and each one of them will get a chance at bat. The objective is to smash that burrito hard enough to send bits of it flying everywhere.

You doing the pitching is very deliberate. First, you want to give really easy pitches to the kids so that they get good hits. You can do that best. And second, for the illustration of this, you want some of the burrito bits to hit you. You'll tie that in later. And with that goal in mind, be sure to stand close enough to the batter to make that happen.

When the kids miss, pick up that burrito and pitch it again. You really want each of the kids to get the fun of connecting. By the time all of the kids get a turn at bat, you should have a nice, big mess. Excellent! Great job!

Don't clean up just yet. At this point you'll want to move on to hit the point of the lesson.

Teaching the Lesson

Well, making the burritos explode was fun, wasn't it? Burrito baseball definitely made a mess, but there's no real harm done. But today we want to talk about anger. When people explode in anger, it often makes a very different kind of mess—one that is a lot harder to clean up than this one will be. What makes explosions of anger so messy?

- Some people say really nasty, hurtful things when they get angry, things that others aren't likely to forget for a long, long time.
- Some people do some really destructive, foolish things when they get angry, things that are impossible to undo.

In the Bible, we read a number of tragic stories of how outbursts of anger made messes. King Saul wrestled with jealous anger. In one of his outbursts in 1 Samuel 18, he threw a spear at David, hoping to kill him. David dodged the throw. Then it happened again in the very next chapter. David had seen enough of the king's anger and decided it was time to leave for good. He had been one of the king's most loyal men and an absolutely lethal commander in the king's army, defeating the king's enemies. Because of his explosions of anger, King Saul lost a really, really good man.

That same King Saul got really angry at his own son, Jonathan, and guess what? He threw a spear at him too. Jonathan dodged it, but he saw his dad differently from that point. He lost respect for his dad. In both of these cases, Saul's anger made a mess that hurt him—and others.

In the book of Exodus, we see Pharoah's pride and hard-heartedness . . . and his anger at Moses. In his anger he refused to do as God told him to do through Moses. His anger made a huge mess, severely hurting his own country and his own people. In the end, in another rush of anger, he had his army chase Moses and the escaping Hebrews. The entire army was swallowed up by the Red Sea, and every soldier drowned.

We could also talk about King Nebuchadnezzar, and how his anger caused him to heat up the fiery furnace seven times hotter than normal, resulting in the death of some of his best men.

Well, I'm wearing some of the burritos, aren't I? That's a reminder that outbursts of anger make life messier for us—and those closest to us. So often our anger is just foolish, and it does great damage.

> Fools give full vent to their rage,
>> but the wise bring calm in the end. (Prov. 29:11)

Summing It Up

Anger isn't something that just goes away as we grow older. We've all seen way too many crabby old people. Anger is usually destructive, and we want to get away from those kinds of outbursts, don't we?

Talk to God about it in prayer. Ask him to help you. Confess when you mess up, and give him permission to change your heart. And when you feel yourself getting angry, start praying again that God will help you.

> A hot-tempered person stirs up conflict,
>> but the one who is patient calms a quarrel. (15:18)

With God's help, we don't have to be the kind of person who makes messes with our anger. We can actually be the kind of person who calms things down, one who keeps messes from happening in the first place. That's the kind of person I want to be . . . and I hope you want to be as well.

> My dear brothers and sisters, take note of this: Everyone should be quick to listen, slow to speak and slow to become angry, because human anger does not produce the righteousness that God desires. (James 1:19–20)

I Wouldn't Say That

Talking rudely to others is not okay with God.

THINGS YOU'LL NEED

☐ Prize for the winner(s). The game show questions (included below) are obvious, so likely you'll have a tie for the win. The prize might be something you can all enjoy as a family. Pizza? Ice cream? Just make your plan so you can announce it before starting the game show.

Advance Prep

Look over the "game show" questions. If some aren't age appropriate for your kids, cross them out. Don't hesitate to add your own questions.

It seems like people are less kind and more rude than ever. We see so much of that on social media. People often express their opinions and criticisms in mean, nasty, and downright caustic ways. Exercising kindness in the way we talk to others—especially with those we disagree with—is becoming a lost verbal art. Hopefully you'll be able to change that a bit after today, at least in your own family.

Running the Activity

Get the kids together and introduce the "I Wouldn't Say That" game show. Ideally, you'll have two play this game. If you've got more kids, the others make up the audience. If you have one child present, that works too.

Explain how the "I Wouldn't Say That" game show works.

1. You'll list some categories, and your contestant will select one.
2. You'll read a question or statement from that category. The answer is simply either "I would say that," or "I wouldn't say that." The obvious right answer for all the questions, by the way, is "I wouldn't say that." If they give the right answer (and they should), give them a point. If they give the wrong answer, realize they may be messing with you a bit. Just roll with it.

Run the game only as long as you need. Five minutes should be plenty. Three minutes may be better. Don't go too long; they'll lose interest. If each contestant has the chance to answer four questions, that should be plenty to drive home the point of today's lesson.

> The statements are ridiculous, for the most part. Explain to the kids that they're intended to be said loudly as a joke or to be funny. And the question for the kids is simply . . . "Would you say that?"

Category: At the Airport

1. Wow, this backpack is heavy. I never knew a bomb could weigh so much!
2. I have no idea what's in this suitcase. Some stranger outside gave me $50 to check it on the plane with my luggage.

Category: At the Bank

1. Give me all the cash in the drawer.
2. This is a holdup.

Category: In a School

1. Sometimes I get so angry, I could shoot someone!
2. Those kids have made me feel stupid too many times. Very soon they'll be sorry. Yeah, they'll all be sorry!
3. I could use some fresh air. I think I'll go pull a fire alarm.

Category: At a Restaurant

1. I think I just saw a rat run out of the kitchen!
2. There's a worm in my salad!
3. There's a wad of hair in my soup!

Category: At the Dinner Table

1. Whoever cooked this meal must be a total idiot. This is the worst meal I've ever had!
2. I was talking to a friend today. We're thinking of dropping out of school and joining a traveling carnival after we get our driver's licenses.
3. We just completed a unit in health class about the dangers of drugs. I don't know if I buy all the paranoid warnings. I mean,

how can you really say those drugs are bad unless you've tried them?

Category: To Your Boss

1. Wow, I love this job. I just got back from a little nap in the stockroom. I get paid to sleep!
2. My friends love the fact that I work at a fast-food restaurant. They're always coming in to get more free food.
3. I borrowed a little money from the cash register. That's okay, yeah? I did that all the time at my other job—and I was pretty good about paying most of it back too.

Category: Guy Talking to the Parent of the Girl He's Taking on a First Date

1. You have a curfew for your daughter? I usually stay out as late as I want with other girls.
2. I'll try to have her home on time, but I'm almost out of gas, and I don't get my allowance for another week. If we run out of gas, we'll walk back as quickly as we can.

Category: Girl Talking to the Parent of the Boy She's Taking on a First Date

1. My one dream is that I get married and have a baby before I graduate from high school.
2. I really don't want to go out with your son. I'm just doing it to make my ex-boyfriend jealous.

Category: A Doctor Talking to a Patient Just before Surgery

1. This is a relatively simple surgery, which is fortunate. I haven't tried it in years.

2. We'll be trying a new surgical procedure on you today. In fact, I was just reading about it yesterday and said, "Gee, I have to try this technique on someone."

3. Hey, be happy you get to sleep during surgery today. I was up partying all night. I could fall asleep standing up!

4. Let's hope this week is a better week for surgery. Last week I messed up on every single one.

Category: A Nurse in a Maternity Ward

1. Uh-oh. I shouldn't have taken the name bands off. Which baby is which?

2. If there was a prize for "World's Ugliest Baby," your baby would take first place!

Category: A Teacher Talking to Parents at a School Open House or Parents Co-op

1. The truth is, I really hate kids.

2. Yes, I have my favorite students, and I treat them well. Too bad your kid isn't one of them.

Category: Posting on Social Media

1. It's okay to say anything you want about somebody on social media. If I think they're a jerk, what's wrong with me telling my friends?

2. It's okay to call somebody names on social media. It's a free country, right?

3. It's okay to say some pretty nasty things about others if they've said rude things about you.

4. It's okay to post mean things about somebody else if they're true. I'm a truth-teller; isn't that what Christians are supposed to do?

5. It's okay to make fun of somebody on social media. Hey, they're the one who did the stupid thing. I'm just telling all my friends about it.

6. It's okay to say mean things about someone online—as long as you don't put it in all caps, because that would be rude.

Okay, tally up the score. Hopefully the kids got the answers right, and they've earned the prize. Now move on to the lesson, but be careful not to draw it out too long. My guess? Your kids probably already got the point of this lesson, so keep it moving.

Teaching the Lesson

By the way you scored on our little game show, you've proven you have good common sense when it comes to knowing what to say— and what *not* to say. If we say the wrong thing at the wrong time or place, it could cause lots of pain and problems.

We did good with the game . . . but how about in real life? Sometimes we say or do things to siblings or parents that are not kind. They're rude. Sometimes we do the same things to others outside our family or our group of friends. I'm not going to give any specific examples, but I'll just mention some things in general.

- Telling someone they're stupid in a non-joking way.
- Interrupting a younger sibling like they're not important or as if what they have to say doesn't matter.
- Talking fresh to parents—or behind their back when you think they won't hear you.
- Making fun of people who make a mistake.
- Making fun of people for how they look, dress, act, or talk.
- Expressing your opinions about others in ways that are overly critical and hurtful.

- Talking only about yourself in a conversation and not being interested in what the other person may have to share.
- Being critical, rude, sarcastic, or mean on social media.

We could probably add to this list, but you get the idea. Here's the thing:

1. Jesus told us that we're to love others.

> A new command I give you: Love one another. As I have loved you, so you must love one another. By this everyone will know that you are my disciples, if you love one another. (John 13:34–35)

2. Love is not rude. Love is kind.

> Love is patient and kind; love does not envy or boast; it is not arrogant or rude. It does not insist on its own way; it is not irritable or resentful; it does not rejoice at wrongdoing, but rejoices with the truth. Love bears all things, believes all things, hopes all things, endures all things. (1 Cor. 13:4–7 ESV)

There are many more Bible verses to back those two statements up, but I think those did the job. When we are being rude and unkind, we are not obeying Jesus. When we're disobeying Jesus, we're sinning. Not good.

Summing It Up

Sometimes people say they're only telling the truth, but it's just a way of excusing themselves for being rude. And the thing is, if we were more careful with what we say, we'd save ourselves from a lot of hard things.

> Those who guard their mouths and their tongues
> keep themselves from calamity. (Prov. 21:23)

One more thought. If we find ourselves saying rude things instead of kind things and mean things instead of nice things, or if we find ourselves tearing people down instead of building them up, the problem may be with us . . . not just others. Jesus pointed out that whatever fills our hearts is what comes out of our mouths.

> For out of the abundance of the heart the mouth speaks. (Matt. 12:34 ESV)

I think it would be good for all of us to work at being kind with the things we say to and about others. And if we're having real trouble doing that, we need to work on it. We start by confessing that we've messed up in that area, and then we ask God to help us be more kind with the things we say to and about others. Often, we just need a change of perspective—a change of heart. Let's give the Holy Spirit permission to work in our hearts to make us less rude or nasty and more kind instead.

Our Ruler's Two Rules

THEME: God's love is amazing, yet some see God as being primarily about creating rules we must follow. Excessive rules and laws describe the world we live in much more than how God operates.

THINGS YOU'LL NEED

☐ A field trip to the library—or a lawyer's office. Anywhere you can bring the kids to show them shelves and shelves of law books.

Advance Prep

You'll want to go to the library ahead of time to see if they've got shelves of law books. Real estate law. Business law. Government law. If you don't see much of a selection, you might try a lawyer's office, unless they access everything online. Ideally, you want the kids to see the physical comparison: one Bible versus many volumes of law books.

Also, you can Google the number of law books in the Library of Congress. When I did that, the answer was 2.9 *million*. That's a staggering number, for sure.

Running the Activity

Bring the kids to see some law books at the library or a lawyer's office. Take out a volume and carefully flip through it so they see how much text is on a page and how many laws there really are. You might have the kids actually count the number of law books on the shelves. That will really help drive this point home.

Now you can take the kids home, to a fast-food restaurant, or wherever to help them catch the nugget of truth found in this lesson.

Teaching the Lesson

Sometimes people complain about God. They see him as a stern judge. A demanding ruler. One who creates countless rules and laws that he absolutely expects us to follow—or else! People even joke about how God might zap someone who steps out of line somehow.

People point to the Bible as "Exhibit A." They claim that the Bible is just a bunch of dos and don'ts—as if that is proof that God rules his universe with nothing but rules.

The Bible isn't cover-to-cover rules, is it? It contains a number of rules for living, absolutely. Much of that is needed so people can live in a society that is safe for everyone. But there is much more to the Bible than just rules or laws. The Bible is filled with history. Stories of heroes and villains. Stories of war and peace. Stories of ordinary people who did extraordinary things—with God's help.

The Bible also contains lots and lots of wisdom on how to live a life that brings peace and satisfaction and is meaningful. There are letters of encouragement in the Bible. Songs of praise to God. The Bible teaches us how to relate to others.

The Bible ultimately tells us about God's great love for us—and how Jesus paid the price for our sins so we can be saved. God gave us the Bible to show us how we can know him and be spared from the penalty of our own sins.

> But because of his great love for us, God, who is rich in mercy, made us alive with Christ even when we were dead in transgressions—it is by grace you have been saved. (Eph. 2:4–5)

Is God just a rule-slinging ruler—and the Bible simply a book of dos and don'ts? Hardly. In fact, Jesus boiled all the laws of the Bible down to two.

> One of them, an expert in the law, tested him with this question: "Teacher, which is the greatest commandment in the Law?"
>
> Jesus replied: "'Love the Lord your God with all your heart and with all your soul and with all your mind.' This is the first and greatest commandment. And the second is like it: 'Love your neighbor as yourself.' All the Law and the Prophets hang on these two commandments." (Matt. 22:35–40)

So, two commandments make up the entire foundation for all the "rules" God has created for us. Compare that to the world we live in. In fact, the "dos and don'ts" accusation fits a whole lot better with the way the world operates rather than describing God, the Bible, and Christianity.

How many law books did we see at the library today?

And there are many more law books than what we saw. When I Googled "Number of law books in the Library of Congress," does anybody want to guess how many books are shelved there? There are 2.9 *million*!

God's two laws . . . versus 2.9 million law books in our nation alone! Law books are filled with restrictions and legal rights—and what happens to people who break those laws or boundaries. The law books have nothing to do with showing love. They are about keeping people in line and listing the consequences they'll face if they don't obey! Our God is so different from that. Yes, God has laws and boundaries and penalties recorded in the Bible. But the loving heart of God is reflected throughout the whole Bible. God created the Bible to show us how to be freed from the penalty of sin . . . the penalty of breaking those laws.

> Jesus performed many other signs in the presence of his disciples, which are not recorded in this book. But these are written that you may believe that Jesus is the Messiah, the Son of God, and that by believing you may have life in his name. (John 20:30–31)

The verses above tell us that whole parts of the Bible are written just so we can be free. That's amazing! God gave us the Bible so we wouldn't live a wasted life and spend eternity in hell. There is no law book in the world written with that intent.

Summing It Up

Some people say God is very restrictive. But we've just seen how that is a better description of the world system than of God or the Bible or Christianity.

It makes me wonder how the accusation that "the Bible is just dos and don'ts" even got started. I wonder if it was the devil himself who got that ball rolling. He'd do just about anything to keep people from opening the Bible and discovering what is *really* in there—and what God is really like—don't you think? I hope you do open your Bible and discover the treasure and truth inside.

And the next time somebody tries to convince you that God, the Bible, or Christianity is all about a bunch of rules, I hope you don't fall for that line. In fact, tell them the truth by using the comparison we mentioned about God's two laws . . . versus the 2.9 million *books* of laws found in the Library of Congress.

Higher Flier

THEME: We can't work our way into heaven, no matter how good we are.

 THINGS YOU'LL NEED

- ☐ Model rocket kit. Available at hobby stores or online (check EstesRock ets.com). If you can pick up one rocket for each of the kids, terrific. Otherwise, one per family will do. Some rockets require assembly, so keep that in mind when purchasing. My suggestion? Go with a "no assembly" or "easy assembly" choice.
- ☐ Model rocket launcher. Sold separately, or often with a starter rocket kit.
- ☐ Model rocket engine(s). Engines are single-use, so you'll use one engine for each flight. Every rocket will state on the box what size engine it takes: A, B, C, etc. The higher the letter, the more power it has. "C" engines will shoot the rockets higher than "A" engines. If you've never done this before, stick with A or B. If your rocket goes

too high, the wind will carry it, and your chances of losing it will go sky-high.

☐ Safety glasses for all who will be present at the launch

Advance Prep

You'll need to assemble the rocket(s) in advance. Sometimes there are parts to glue, and they'll need time to dry. Even if no assembly is required, you'll want to pull the rocket out and read the instructions. Sometimes the parachute needs to be fitted inside the rocket.

It's your call, but you may want to get the kids involved in the building process. Often there are stickers to affix to the rocket, and they can customize the thing to make it look the way they want. It will also build anticipation for the real launch day when you're having family devotions.

Find a good site for launching the rocket(s). A big, open field works nice. These rockets go pretty high, and if there is a breeze, the wind can carry them quite a distance away.

Test this on your own *before* trying it with the kids. You'll be much, much smoother during devotions time if you've made a practice run. That will also give you a chance to get familiar with the launcher.

Concerns about doing this alone? Ask around at church. I'll bet you'll find a couple people there who have flown these rockets—and would love to come for your test flight.

Running the Activity

Bring the kids, rockets, launcher, and safety glasses to the launch site. Have them put on the safety glasses right away. Be sure to go over with each of the kids all the safety rules that come with the rocket/launcher or are posted on the manufacturer's website.

Keep the direction of the wind in mind when selecting where to place the launchpad. You may want to angle the launchpad into the breeze so the rocket will drift back over you after the parachute opens.

You may want to have a countdown each time you launch. It helps keep all the kids aware of the fact that the rocket is going to fire off the stand as well. Most launch kits come with a push-button "ignition" switch on a wire or remote so you can launch from a safer distance. The kids will love pressing the button when you give them the go for launch.

Be sure everyone is watching the rocket as it flies skyward. It's easy to lose track of it if you don't keep your eyes on the thing.

If the area is safe enough, you can let the kids chase and retrieve the rocket as it drops back to earth.

With the rocket back in your hands, remove the old engine and set a new one in place—but watch the clock. It takes time to get the rocket ready to fire again. So you may want to send up a second flight right away, or simply teach the devotion first, then enjoy sending up more flights afterward.

Teaching the Lesson

One flight may go higher than the others depending on the wind or the engine we install, but if our goal is to shoot this rocket all the way to the moon, we'll never make it.

It's sort of like getting to heaven. Some people may do great things or good things, or may appear to be "better" than others, but nobody is good enough to make it to heaven on their own.

For all have sinned and fall short of the glory of God. (Rom. 3:23)

Notice those words "fall short." That sort of sounds like our rocket, doesn't it? Any attempt to fly it to the moon will result in the rocket falling far short of the goal. And the same applies to us. Any attempt to make it to heaven based on our own goodness or abilities will fall far short as well.

Summing It Up

The only way our little rocket will make it to the moon is if an astronaut packs it in a *real* rocket. And that's the way it is with us and heaven. No matter how good we are—or think we are—the only way we'll get to heaven is through Jesus.

After our rocket fell back to earth, what did we do? We picked it up and got it ready for another flight.

Jesus is like that too. Sometimes as Christians we are flying high one moment and doing a nosedive the next. We mess up in some way, and we sin. But Jesus knows where we're at. He'll pick us up, clean us off, and fix us so we can fly again. And someday, when our time on earth is through, our Jesus will make sure we get all the way to heaven too!

A Special Word for Parents

If your kids haven't made a decision to follow Christ, this would be a great time to talk to them about it. Or maybe they have friends who have yet to follow Christ. Talk to your kids about using this rocket illustration to explain the gospel to their friends.

Keeping Score

THEME: Forgiving, especially those in our own family, instead of keeping a list of wrongs.

THINGS YOU'LL NEED

- ☐ Trip to a nearby miniature golf (putt-putt) course. Or save this one for a vacation. Touristy spots often have really great, theme-based courses.
- ☐ Prize for the winner. Get creative here. Maybe it's going out for a snack with the family afterward—and the winner ends up winning that prize for the whole family to enjoy.

Advance Prep

No advance prep other than to locate the miniature golf course and decide on the prize.

Running the Activity

Take the family to play miniature golf and just have a great time. Make sure you have a scorecard. At each hole, be sure you or one of the kids gets the score from each player and writes it down. This needs to be a deliberate thing so all the kids are aware that you're keeping careful score. Asking each player by name for their total strokes at each hole is a great way to do that.

You may find some of the kids have a real scorekeeping tendency even as the game progresses. They're the ones who correct the scores given by siblings at the various holes . . . often pointing out that there were some strokes that weren't counted but should have been.

After the game, tally up the scorecard to determine who the winner is. But rather than adding the numbers as they are, do some changes to the totals by lowering some of the numbers—but only for one of the players. Ideally, not the youngest player, or anyone with whom the others may be inclined to overlook what you're doing. Be obvious about it. "I see (*name*) got a score of six on this hole. That can't be right. Before we add things up to see who won, I'm changing that to a three. And on this hole . . . I'm moving it from a five to a two. Here's another one . . . I think we're going to lower that score too."

Basically, you'll want to do something like that long enough to get some serious "that's not fair" protests from the others. And you'll want to change the score enough that it impacts who wins or loses.

Now add up the altered totals and determine your winner. The kids may not like that one bit, but take them out for the prize anyway.

You're all set to talk about this over the food/snacks you picked up.

Teaching the Lesson

When I lowered some of the tallies at various holes, most of you didn't like that very much, right? Keeping accurate score in a miniature golf game is important. But there are times in family life when we tend to keep score—and it is a really bad thing. I'm talking about when we keep a mental list of the "wrongs" others in the family do.

Things like keeping track of how much more work you do, or how many jobs Mom or Dad has given you compared to what others in the family are doing. Or maybe you're keeping track of how often your brother or sister messes up in some way. Maybe it is simply the number of times they annoy you—or things they do that "wrong" you.

This type of keeping score is common in families, but that isn't the way God wants it to be. Check out these verses from the famous passage in the Bible that describes what real love is like:

> Love is patient, love is kind. It does not envy, it does not boast, it is not proud. It does not dishonor others, it is not self-seeking, it is not easily angered, **it keeps no record of wrongs**. (1 Cor. 13:4–5, emphasis added)

So, the Bible tells us we're to love others, and it also shows us what love looks like. If I'm keeping a mental list of wrongs about others in the family—and calling attention to them when I think something is unfair or I want something done my way—I'm messing up.

Keeping a list of wrongs can be really, really destructive. We can damage our relationships when we act like a human scorecard, remembering each other's mess-ups and shortcomings.

In Luke 10:38–42 we have the account of two sisters, Mary and Martha. Martha was a scorekeeper type of person.

> As Jesus and his disciples were on their way, he came to a village where a woman named Martha opened her home to him. She had a sister called Mary, who sat at the Lord's feet listening to what he said. But Martha was distracted by all the preparations that had to be made. She came to him and asked, "Lord, don't you care that my sister has left me to do the work by myself? Tell her to help me!"

"Martha, Martha," the Lord answered, "you are worried and upset about many things, but few things are needed—or indeed only one. Mary has chosen what is better, and it will not be taken away from her."

Martha was keeping score. She was the one doing all the work around there, while Mary was doing nothing. So, when Martha couldn't stand it any longer, she complained to Jesus about her sister. Basically, she resorted to tattling. Of course that didn't go very well, because Jesus corrected Martha and pointed out that the real problem was with her. *Ouch.*

Jesus himself was often confronted by people who kept a list of his "wrongs." The Pharisees were huge with this. They felt Jesus was wrong to hang around people who were sinners. They felt Jesus was wrong to heal on the Sabbath. They felt Jesus was wrong when he didn't follow their little traditions—and didn't make his disciples follow them either. Silly things like not washing their hands properly. The Pharisees sound absolutely ridiculous, don't they?

That's what happens when we keep a list of wrongs. We look petty. Whiny. It's not the stuff of mature Christian believers but of the really, really immature.

Summing It Up

Keeping a list of wrongs is not demonstrating love at all. It's really selfish. Proud. And ultimately ungrateful. The fact that Jesus has forgiven our sins and doesn't keep a list of wrongs should make us so grateful that we show that same grace and mercy to others by losing the list of wrongs we keep on them.

Jesus pointed out that we need to forgive over and over again.

Then Peter came to Jesus and asked, "Lord, how many times shall I forgive my brother or sister who sins against me? Up to seven times?"

Jesus answered, "I tell you, not seven times, but seventy-seven times." (Matt. 18:21–22)

Jesus forgives us over and over . . . and we need to do the same for others. Especially those right in our own family.

Ultimately, keeping a list of wrongs will hurt relationships. In a family. Between friends. In a marriage. When we remember the things others have done to "wrong" or hurt us—and we bring them up again and again—how can that do anything but weaken our relationship with them? That kind of behavior hurts us, because people won't want to be around us all that much. And it certainly hurts others when we bring up their so-called shortcomings, doesn't it?

When we find ourselves criticizing a brother or sister with a sentence that starts with "You never," or "You always," it's a pretty good guess that we're keeping a list of wrongs.

Instead of doing that, let's get in the practice of overlooking things others do that annoy us. Love doesn't keep a list of wrongs . . . it blots that list out. It paints over it.

> Whoever would foster love covers over an offense,
> but whoever repeats the matter separates close friends.
> (Prov. 17:9)

Sometimes we may need to talk to the person who wrongs us some way. But we'll want to do that in a really kind way if we expect to get good results. And then after we've done that . . . we can forget about it. Rip up the scorecard. Cover it over. If we do that—with God's help—we'll have a lot less pain ourselves in life—and we'll do a lot less damage to family members and friends, and all those we care most about. Family life and friendships are so much better when we learn to stop keeping score.

A Special Word for Parents

Mom and Dad . . . this is a really essential lesson to teach. But there's one more thing you may want to cover, especially if the kids are ten years old and over. **Forgiving someone over and over doesn't mean tolerating abuse.** If they feel someone is abusing them, they aren't to just stay silent and keep taking it. They need to talk to someone and get help.

And another important aspect you'll want to cover has to do with trust. We may forgive someone over and over . . . that is loving. But the Scripture passages don't require us to restore that other person to full trust. We surely don't want our kids taken advantage of by someone who is habitually mistreating them or is downright abusive. It is important to teach our kids that trust can be broken, and we don't simply reward that person by giving trust back. That will have to be earned.

For example, if a friend borrows money and promises to repay it—but they never do? We can forgive that debt but not feel obligated to keep making loans to them. Help your kids understand how to forgive and how not to hold a grudge . . . absolutely. But just as important, free them from the obligation to reward the other person with their trust again. Do these two things, and you'll be giving them a valuable lesson about life.

Riding on Rails

THEME: Loving God and loving others are like two rails that help keep us on track in this Christian life.

THINGS YOU'LL NEED

☐ A train ride with the family—maybe a trip into the city or to a nearby town.

Advance Prep

There's no other prep beyond figuring out the train details. Also be thinking about the destination. Is there a restaurant, museum, or something fun to do where you get off the train?

Running the Activity

You might take a moment to look at the tracks with the kids before you board. Then simply enjoy the train ride—and do everything you can to make the ride fun for the kids. Part of the secret to this is what you'll do when you get to your destination. A restaurant, store, or a museum they'd like are all possibilities. You're not trying to make the trip just educational, though. The idea is for it to be fun. So, whatever says fun to them . . . that's what you'll want to do.

Now, you can teach the lesson part of this before you reboard the train to go home or after you get home. Either way works. If you can do it before you reboard, the kids may think about what you said a bit more on the ride back.

Teaching the Lesson

Trains have been around for a couple hundred years—and there have been plenty of things that have changed. How they look. How they're powered. But there's one thing that hasn't changed. Can anybody guess what that is?

Trains still run on a set of tracks. Two steel rails running parallel with each other.

What happens if the wheels on the train slip off the track? It would be a disaster. Trains aren't designed to run on a single rail. To be balanced—to go anywhere safely—the train needs to ride squarely on both rails.

There is a parallel to the Christian life here. As Christians, we run on tracks too. To be balanced, to keep from being derailed in some way, we need two rails in our Christian life. Jesus made that pretty clear when he was asked what the single most important commandment was.

Jesus replied: "'Love the Lord your God with all your heart and with all your soul and with all your mind.' This is the first and greatest commandment. And the second is like it: 'Love your neighbor as yourself.' All the Law and the Prophets hang on these two commandments." (Matt. 22:37–40)

Love God . . . and love others. Jesus made it clear that these are the two things that should guide all that we do.

Love God. We're not talking about just some warm fuzzy feeling we get. Loving God—loving Jesus—is all about obeying him. If we aren't doing what the Bible says, these verses show us that we truly don't love him.

Jesus replied, "Anyone who loves me will obey my teaching. My Father will love them, and we will come to them and make our home with them. Anyone who does not love me will not obey my teaching. These words you hear are not my own; they belong to the Father who sent me." (John 14:23–24)

But if anyone obeys his word, love for God is truly made complete in them. This is how we know we are in him: Whoever claims to live in him must live as Jesus did. (1 John 2:5–6)

Love others. This goes hand in hand with loving God. To say we love God—but then to treat some of his kids in unkind ways? That doesn't really sound like we love God as he'd want us to, does it? Jesus put it this way:

A new command I give you: Love one another. As I have loved you, so you must love one another. By this everyone will know that you are my disciples, if you love one another. (John 13:34–35)

Summing It Up

If someone says they love God or love Jesus, but they aren't obeying what the Bible says, they aren't truly loving God or Jesus at all.

If someone says they're a follower of Jesus, yet they are unloving toward others, they are not obeying Jesus at all. Jesus said we must love others. And we've already seen that if we aren't obeying Jesus, our love for him is not real.

Lots of Christians may *say* they love God, but when they treat people in mean or unkind ways, that proves their love for God is pretty shallow or immature.

Loving God. Loving others. If we want to keep our lives from derailing—from becoming a train wreck—we need to stay on this track. This is the path Jesus laid out for us. We need to keep our wheels on these two rails. As long as we do, we're in for a great ride!

Fun Flamethrower

THEME: Christians have a responsibility to be a good example to others, especially to those who are younger—even brothers and sisters.

 THINGS YOU'LL NEED

- ☐ Plastic spray bottle with an adjustable nozzle to make a fine mist. (Buy a new one at the grocery or hardware store. They're cheap, and you want to make sure there was no other combustible chemical inside it before.)
- ☐ Taper candle, 8" tall or more
- ☐ Wire hanger
- ☐ Duct tape
- ☐ Matches or lighter
- ☐ Rubbing alcohol, at least ½ quart
- ☐ Safety glasses for all present

☐ Bucket of water and/or hose

☐ Optional: wire snips

Advance Prep

The supplies list and advance prep look detailed—and you might be tempted to skip this one. Don't. The supplies are super cheap, and the assembly instructions only look long because I'm trying to make them clear and easy.

Or maybe you're thinking of skipping this because you're worried about the fire. You're afraid you're going to give the kids bad ideas. Actually, that's a huge reason *to* do this. This object lesson makes the point of the lesson so clear. Really, you can do this safely . . . and the kids will love it. That means they'll remember the important theme of the lesson too. And there is no better way to teach your kids to be a good example to younger ones than by doing something that might be seen as kind of dangerous.

Still on the fence? Okay. Just assemble the flamethrower and try it outdoors on your own. When you do, you'll break out in a huge smile. You'll know how well this will work for the kids, and any reservations you have will vanish.

Now, let's make a little flamethrower.

1. Untwist the hanger to make one long wire. Wrap one end several times around the neck of the spray bottle and secure it in place with the duct tape.

2. Coil the other end of the wire around the shaft of the taper candle and secure it with duct tape. The candle should be positioned upright about 8″ from the nozzle of the spray bottle. Use the wire snips to cut off any excess hanger wire or loop it

back to the spray bottle to reinforce that arm extending to the candle.

3. Bend the wire arm extending from the sprayer to the candle so that the candle tip/wick is just an inch or two (horizontally) below the nozzle—but still 8″ away.

4. Pour a few ounces of rubbing alcohol into the spray bottle and screw the nozzle back on tight.

   Now, you'll absolutely need to test this before doing it with the kids. **Take the entire spray bottle/candle assembly outside.** Be sure you have a bucket of water at your feet and/or a running hose. And this is the time to put on your safety glasses, my friend.

5. Before lighting the candle, adjust the spray nozzle to be sure the rubbing alcohol comes out in a fine mist. **Turn the nozzle away from the candle before you do this.** Coating the entire candle with rubbing alcohol before lighting it wouldn't be the smartest choice right now.

6. Realign the candle. Then light it and, making sure there is nothing in front of you that could catch fire, give the spray bottle a pump. The rubbing alcohol mist should ignite as it passes the flame, creating a momentary—but impressive—burst of flame. Play with it until you get a consistent burst each time. Usually bending the wire to raise the candle a bit will do the trick.

Fun, right? And the kids will love it too. Now, disassemble the flamethrower if you think the kids will enjoy building it with you—or just leave it intact, and you're ready to go. Either way, be sure to empty all of the rubbing alcohol from the spray bottle so the thing is completely nonfunctional until you're ready to do this with the kids.

Running the Activity

Take the kids outside for the little flamethrower demo. Doing this at night is even more fun, if that's possible. Be sure all the safety elements are in place.

- Bucket of water and/or hose
- Safety glasses on all present
- Nothing in the path of the flame

Depending on the ages of the kids and what you feel is appropriate, let each of them have a turn making those bursts of flame. Keep a close eye on each one to make sure they're handling it safely and pointing it in the right direction. Maybe someone can catch some pictures or video with your phone. Now, blow out the candle. You're all set up to teach the nugget of truth for this lesson.

Teaching the Lesson

Okay, this was fun—but it could be dangerous too, couldn't it? Especially if someone younger tried to imitate what you were doing.

KEEP IT SAFE

You may want to remind the kids that the flamethrower isn't a toy. It is something you'll keep—and you can't have them sneaking it out and playing with it. If they decide to do that anyway, explain that as a consequence you won't be able to do the dangerous devotionals with them. You'll have to stick with the tamer ones, which is not something they'd want you to do. Be sure they know that you'll take the flamethrower out anytime they want to show it to a friend—or want to see it demonstrated. I would take the flamethrower apart at this point and tuck everything away so they aren't tempted.

Imagine what might happen if they tried this indoors. What might happen if they did this by a set of drapes?

What kind of responsibility do you have to be a good example for younger brothers or sisters—or other kids in general? If they do something wrong or dangerous because they saw you do it, what level of blame do you share in that? Check out these verses.

If anyone causes one of these little ones—those who believe in [Jesus]—to stumble, it would be better for them to have a large mill-stone hung around their neck and to be drowned in the depths of the sea. Woe to the world because of the things that cause people to stumble! Such things must come, but woe to the person through whom they come! (Matt. 18:6–7)

It's clear that we have a responsibility to be a good example, whether we want that responsibility or not.

What are some wrong things older brothers or sisters might do that their younger siblings might imitate? Things that might cause them to get in trouble, to sin, to be in danger, or to stumble in some way?

- Talking disrespectfully to or about parents.
- Driving fast or recklessly (if you have any kids with a driver's license).
- Watching or playing unwholesome music, movies, or video games.
- Secretly sinning and hiding it . . . like viewing pornography.
- Treating others without honor or respect (especially in terms of boys and girls).
- Holding grudges.
- Getting even.
- Being dishonest.

- Erupting in angry outbursts.
- Arguing.
- Being selfish and having an "it's all about me" attitude.
- Being arrogant or proud.
- Being unkind.
- Putting others down or gossiping.

You can likely add to this list. But the Bible is clear: we have a responsibility to live in such a way that we don't cause others to stumble. We may not like it—and it may not always feel fair—but that's how God set things up.

And when you think about it, his plan makes a ton of sense. Younger kids don't have as much experience and will often try to imitate those who are older. It's part of human nature. When you were younger, you probably tried to act like some of the older kids you knew as well. And God expects those who are older not to think only of themselves but also about how their choices will impact others.

Don't you love how God is always looking to protect those who are young?

Summing It Up

There are things that may be okay for us to do but would be too dangerous for someone younger to do—such as safely operate our little flamethrower. There are also some things we do that are not okay, and if someone younger imitated us, we could cause them to sin. Sometimes we have to limit our liberty, our freedom, so as not to lead someone else in the wrong direction. The apostle Paul puts it this way:

So whether you eat or drink or whatever you do, do it all for the glory of God. Do not cause anyone to stumble, whether Jews, Greeks or the church of God—even as I try to please everyone in every way. For I am not seeking my own good but the good of many, so that they may be saved. (1 Cor. 10:31–33)

Notice that we're not to be focused so much on what *we* want but on what is best for others. We could handle the flamethrower—but it may have been a bad example to someone younger if they tried imitating us. The whole point of this activity is to remind us that we have to consider others when we make choices. We need to ask ourselves if we might cause someone to stumble if they try imitating us or following the way we talk or act.

It can seem tough or unfair at times. But that is what God is asking us to do as an act of love for him and for others. Let's be a good example in what we do and say . . . and in our attitudes too. Let's make that our hearts' desire, and then let's ask God to help us do exactly that.

Don't let anyone look down on you because you are young, but set an example for the believers in speech, in conduct, in love, in faith and in purity. (1 Tim. 4:12)

If you see an older kid doing something that is a good example for the younger ones—at home or at church—be sure to encourage them along in that area.

Flying Under the Radar

The dangers and ridiculousness of pride.

THINGS YOU'LL NEED

☐ Garden hose and spray attachment or sprinkler
☐ Towels for the kids afterward

Advance Prep

You might want to test the hose with the sprayer/sprinkler to see which one will work best for the kids. The sprinkler has a nice advantage because the water hitting your kids won't be as concentrated—so there's less chance of tears caused by the stream hitting them in the ears or eyes.

If you're using a sprinkler, you'll want it to simply spray in one spot instead of oscillating, if possible. That will make it a bit easier to use.

Running the Activity

Take the kids outside and show how you're going to hold the sprayer/sprinkler to make a horizontal stream. Each of them will take turns passing under the stream of water, trying not to get wet. Now, they can't just duck under it. They'll need to pass under the spray by bending backward, limbo style.

You might tell them to imagine that each of them is a fighter jet making a raid in enemy territory. They'll need to stay below the radar. If they don't, they'll get hit by the water.

Keep the water easily over their heads for their first pass under it as sort of a practice round. But tell them you'll lower the stream of water a little bit each time. If their head catches a blast of water, they're out. You might say that they didn't quite stay below the radar—and the enemy shot them down. Repeat this until everybody has been eliminated except your winner.

You'll want to be careful *not* to spray the kids in the eyes or ears, especially if using a sprayer instead of a sprinkler.

Teaching the Lesson

With some games, it's the person who rises above the rest, the person who stays on top, who is declared the winner. In today's little water game, it was the person who managed to keep their head *low* who won.

And in life, it gets very easy to raise our chins or our heads in pride. We might feel justified in some way. Maybe we did a really good job on something, or we get heady or proud because we possess some skill or talent. But raising our heads in pride is going to make us an easy target for the enemy. Whenever we're proud, we're in trouble. Let's look at some verses from the Bible.

> When pride comes, then comes disgrace,
> but with humility comes wisdom. (Prov. 11:2)

Pride goes before destruction,
a haughty spirit before a fall. (16:18)

For those who exalt themselves will be humbled, and those who humble themselves will be exalted. (Matt. 23:12)

Summing It Up

Sometimes Mom or Dad will say to you, "I'm so proud of you!" or maybe something like, "You did such a great job . . . you should be proud of yourself."

The thing is, if we absorb that praise, likely we'll get proud—which will hurt us. To avoid issues with pride because we did a great job at something or because we have some kind of special skills or abilities, it helps if we remember some key truths.

Who gave us the abilities, looks, health, strength, intelligence, and so on that we have?

Who gave us the opportunity that brought us that praise in the first place?

The answer to both of those questions is God, right? So, when we're feeling proud about who we are or what we've done, that's kind of a ridiculous thing to do. God is the one who deserves the credit. When we're feeling proud about something we've done, we need to remember to thank God. He's the one who deserves all the praise, not us.

Any pilots who fly above the radar in enemy territory are setting themselves up as an easy target for attack—and likely a crash. And so are we, if our hearts are filled with pride. If we raise our heads in pride, we'll be an easy target for the enemy . . . and that isn't a good thing. Our enemy, the devil and his demons, can destroy us with our pride. The consequences of raising our heads in pride will be a whole lot worse than catching a stream of water in the face!

Let's keep our hearts full of gratitude and thanks to God. We can think of all he's done for us—and all he continues to do. We can also think of all the plans he has for our future. And if we do that, there will be no room for pride in our hearts anyway.

> Many, LORD my God,
>   are the wonders you have done,
>   the things you have planned for us.
> None can compare with you;
>   were I to speak and tell of your deeds,
>   they would be too many to declare. (Ps. 40:5)

Protector or Defector?

THEME: We have a duty to protect each other, and people will get hurt or broken if we dodge that responsibility.

THINGS YOU'LL NEED

- ☐ 2 dozen eggs (1 dozen of which will be smashed)
- ☐ Recipe and supplies to make a favorite meal where eggs are needed (such as scrambled eggs, omelets, or French toast)
- ☐ Small plastic bin to transport broken eggs

Advance Prep

Other than picking up the supplies, no other prep is needed.

Running the Activity

Take the kids to the grocery store to pick up the eggs. Open each of the two cartons with the kids to make sure all the eggs look great, with no cracks. At the checkout, be sure to have a separate plastic grocery bag for each of the egg cartons. You'll use one bag for the demo so it contains the mess—making it easier to toss the whole thing in the garbage when the devotional is over.

Back at the car in the grocery store parking lot, remove one carton of eggs from its plastic bag and ask one of the kids to give you a hand holding the bag open. Announce that you'll bring home one dozen eggs in their carton, but the other dozen you're going to bring home in the bag *without* the carton.

With one of the kids holding the bag open, empty the carton of eggs directly into the bag. This goes against your instincts to handle the eggs carefully, but in this case, you definitely want eggs to crack and break to better make your point.

You may want to put this bag of eggs on the floor or in a plastic bin you thought ahead to bring so you don't get egg oozing into the seats or carpet of the car.

When you get home, gather the kids around and have them check the eggs in the bag. Do you have lots of damage? That's perfect. Now compare that to the eggs you brought home in the egg carton.

To help really drive home the point of the importance of protecting others, have the kids help you salvage the broken eggs. Pour the mess into a bowl, and have the kids remove all the shell shrapnel. Picking out the broken bits of shell will get tedious, but we'll tie that in later.

Teaching the Lesson

Okay, so the eggs we brought home in the carton made it home just fine—but the ones without a carton didn't do nearly as well. So that leads to a pretty obvious question. What is the purpose of the egg carton?

An egg carton protects the eggs. These things have been shipped who knows how far, and they made it to the grocery store just fine. But without the protection of the carton, the eggs couldn't even go a few miles without breaking.

Did you know the Bible gives Christians some "egg carton" responsibilities? Not that we're to protect eggs, but we're to protect each other.

> Love is patient, love is kind. It does not envy, it does not boast, it is not proud. It does not dishonor others, it is not self-seeking, it is not easily angered, it keeps no record of wrongs. Love does not delight in evil but rejoices with the truth. It **always protects**, always trusts, always hopes, always perseveres. (1 Cor. 13:4–7, emphasis added)

Like eggs, people are fragile. They can be hurt or broken and damaged easily. As followers of Jesus, we're to love others. And as we see in these verses, one of the duties of love is to look out for others. We're not only to be concerned about ourselves but have a responsibility to protect others too. This includes brothers and sisters. Friends. Even people we don't know.

Does this mean I need to "cover" for others to protect them from getting in trouble somehow? No, that's not what this Scripture passage is saying. In fact, sometimes covering for someone is not only dishonest but actually hurts the person we hope to protect.

Which of these might be ways that God wants us to protect others?

Being a good example of what it looks like to be a follower of Jesus.

Being a good influence, almost working like a conscience to encourage others to do the right things and make good choices.

Lovingly confronting someone who is doing things that are not right or things that are potentially harmful for them.

Being a bodyguard of sorts by doing your part to protect or warn them about others who would hurt them or be a bad influence on them.

Stepping in to encourage them and lift them up after someone else has verbally torn them down in some way.

All of the above.

Can you think of more ways we can protect others?

Summing It Up

That egg carton may not have looked special, but it was designed to do a really important job. Without the protection of that carton, the eggs got damaged, didn't they? In a similar way, we need to remember that God designed us to love others. And a very real part of loving others has to do with protecting them. It's not just a nice thing we do . . . it's a responsibility God gives us.

If we fail to protect others as we should, we'll often make a lot more work for ourselves. Often it will take a lot of time to undo the damage to others that happened because we failed to protect them. We're much better off just protecting others from the start.

If we dodge this responsibility, if we run from it, it's like we're defecting somehow. Let's ask God to help us be protectors, not defectors, okay?

Remember when you had the kids help you pick the broken shells out of the eggs? Now would be a great time to use them to whip up some scrambled eggs (or other breakfast food featuring eggs) for the kids. You might remind the kids that even if they feel broken or crushed in some way by something somebody else did or said, it doesn't mean God can't use them just like he would have if they'd never been hurt.

Boating or Floating

THEME: Compromising the values and principles God has given us will eventually sink us.

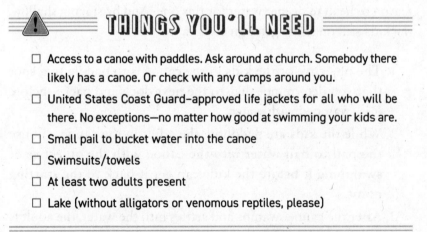

THINGS YOU'LL NEED

- ☐ Access to a canoe with paddles. Ask around at church. Somebody there likely has a canoe. Or check with any camps around you.
- ☐ United States Coast Guard–approved life jackets for all who will be there. No exceptions—no matter how good at swimming your kids are.
- ☐ Small pail to bucket water into the canoe
- ☐ Swimsuits/towels
- ☐ At least two adults present
- ☐ Lake (without alligators or venomous reptiles, please)

Advance Prep

All you really need to do is make arrangements to borrow that canoe and gather the other supplies needed.

Don't try this one without at least two adults on-site. You'll be around water, and more adults present is one way to keep this lesson flowing smoothly and safely all the way. Maybe you can team up with another family. That means more kids, yes, but more adults as well to keep an eye on safety.

Running the Activity

Every one of the kids should be wearing a life jacket if they're on a dock, on the shore, or in the canoe. Make sure every life jacket fits properly and is buckled and strapped securely.

Every run with the canoe should have one adult sitting in the center of the canoe and one or two kids paddling. Plan a route for the canoe that runs parallel to the shore in shallow water. There is no reason to head to deeper water for this one. And by staying shallow, the kids still on shore get a great view.

1. The objective of the kids in the canoe is to paddle to a spot that you determine—like to the next dock and back—before it is swamped with water.
2. While the kids are paddling, the adult in the canoe will use the pail to bail water *into* the canoe with the objective of swamping it before the kids can get it back to the starting point.
3. After the canoe swamps and settles into the water, the adult is to be sure the kids can stand, and together they can drag the canoe to the shore to empty the water and ready it for the next run.

Teaching the Lesson

This canoe activity is a picture of life. As Christians, we're like boats traveling on the troubled waters of this world. We're to be in the world, but the world isn't to be in us. Which is to say we don't remove ourselves from the world and live in isolation somewhere; rather, the world is not to become part of us. We are not to conform to the world.

We're on a journey, a course God has laid out for us—but our enemy, the devil and his demons, wants to keep us from finishing that journey. That was the whole point of adding water to the canoe. That represented how the enemy will try to slow us down, hoping to eventually sink us. Often he does this by filling us with the lies and thinking of the world instead of the truth of God's Word.

Did someone bailing water into the canoe limit how far the canoe could go?

How much water in the canoe did it take before you noticed it was harder to steer the canoe or that you were slowing down?

A canoe is made to float *on* the water, but when you've got water coming *inside*, you've got trouble.

How is the world/our culture different from what God's Word says is good, right, and true?

As Christians, we see the Bible as our guide for truth. For knowing what is right and wrong. What does the world/our culture use as its guide?

As Christians, we know we answer to God for the things we say and do and think. Who do people who are not following Christ feel they answer to?

Don't feel you need to use the whole series of questions here. Read them over in advance and pick the ones that you think might apply best to your kids.

As Christians, we believe that putting the Word into practice leads to a life that pleases God and is fulfilling. How do people who don't follow Christ strive to make their lives fulfilling? And chances are, who are they really trying to please with how they are living?

As Christians, what do we think is the key to happiness versus what people who don't follow Christ think is the key?

How easy is it for the world's thinking . . . the world's values . . . to seep into our lives? How does that happen? Could it come in through social media, TV, internet sources, friends, school, or movies?

Water in the canoe impacted our ability to steer—to get where we needed to go. How might the world seeping into our lives impact us? How might that be slowing us down on our journey with Jesus or making it hard to steer in the right direction and make wise decisions?

If we aren't going in the direction God wants us to travel, how might that affect our relationship with him?

How can we use the truth of God's Word to expose the lies of the world—and to show us how they may be seeping into our lives?

Therefore, I urge you, brothers and sisters, in view of God's mercy, to offer your bodies as a living sacrifice, holy and pleasing to God—this is your true and proper worship. Do not conform to the pattern of this world, but be transformed by the renewing of your mind. Then you will be able to test and approve what God's will is—his good, pleasing and perfect will. (Rom. 12:1–2)

Scripture reminds us here not to conform to the world's ways. We're to resist that. Instead, we're to stay in the Word, which is how we'll transform and renew our minds. That's a great way to stay on course with the plan God has for us.

Summing It Up

Christians are to be in the world, but the world isn't to be in us. That's a big difference. If a boat is taking on water, we find the leak and patch it . . . then we bail like crazy.

In the same way, if the world's attitudes and viewpoints have become part of our lives, we need to see where that is leaking in—and plug that hole. Are there ways that the world's viewpoints are being poured into your life? Sometimes the thinking of this world can seem so right. It makes sense or seems logical. But sometimes what sounds right or logical simply is *not*.

> The house of the wicked will be destroyed,
>> but the tent of the upright will flourish.
>
> There is a way that appears to be right,
>> but in the end it leads to death. (Prov. 14:11–12)

We need to be careful to make sure we are following what God says. Once we've identified areas where the world's thinking has seeped into our lives, we need to do a little mind-renewing by bailing out some of that wrong thinking and replacing it with God's truth. If we don't? We'll soon be just floating in the water, going nowhere, instead of paddling along on the journey God has for us.

> Do not love the world or the things in the world. If anyone loves the world, the love of the Father is not in him. For all that is in the world—the desires of the flesh and the desires of the eyes and pride of life—is not from the Father but is from the world. And the world is passing away along with its desires, but whoever does the will of God abides forever. (1 John 2:15–17 ESV)

Sooner or Later

THEME: Delayed gratification can bring big rewards.

THINGS YOU'LL NEED

- [ ] Very tempting snacks for the kids
- [ ] A $20 IOU written for each of the kids. (Don't worry, you don't have to come up with this money right now—and if this goes as expected, you never will.)
- [ ] $5 bill for each of the kids

Advance Prep

Gather those favorite snacks that your kids will love.

Have the $20 IOUs all written or printed out, one for each of the kids. Be sure to sign and date it. It may say something like, "IOU a

$20 shopping spree for snacks anytime after [put maturity date of two or three months out]."

Write on the margin of each of the $5 bills something like this: "Exchange for $10 bill anytime after [put a maturity date of two or three months out]." If you can afford to make it $20, that would be even better.

Running the Activity

Pick a time when the kids are likely very hungry or when they'd normally have a snack. Lay out all the snacks on the kitchen table and tell the kids you have a deal for them: "You can have this snack now or anytime in the next hour. Or you can wait and hold off on the snack. If you do that, I'll let you go on a $20 snack shopping spree two or three months from now."

Don't show them the IOU certificates or the $5 bills. In fact, now is a good time to leave the room so you aren't influencing their decision at all. Wait a good bit before coming back to finish the lesson. You want to give them time to think about the snack—and time to enjoy eating some if that's their decision.

Teaching the Lesson

Gather up the kids and ask who ate snacks—even a single bite—and who didn't. Those who refrained from eating even a little get their $20 IOU snack certificate. Congratulate them and point out the date it matures. All they have to do is bring it to you anytime after that date to redeem it.

For those who did take snacks, you'll want to display the certificate you'd prepared for them and mark it VOID. They need to see there are benefits to delaying their gratification—and losses when they don't.

In the Bible, we have a story in Genesis 25:19–34 that tells of twin brothers, Esau and Jacob. Esau was born first, so technically he had the "firstborn birthright." This birthright would give him lots and lots of benefits—but not until his dad died.

One day Esau was hungry, and Jacob had a pot of stew cooking. Esau asked for some stew—but Jacob offered him a trade: a bowl of stew in exchange for his firstborn birthright. Esau wanted what he wanted, and he wanted it now. He let his appetite do the thinking instead of his brain. Esau made the deal and gave up his birthright for a bowl of stew. Later, he grew to regret that decision terribly. The birthright was worth infinitely more than one meal. Esau paid a high price because he hadn't learned to wait.

Similar things can happen to us in life.

- Some kids cheat on tests or homework to get a better grade now rather than work and study to gain the knowledge that will truly benefit them later.
- Some kids want to satisfy their sexual appetites now rather than wait for God's plan of sex exclusively reserved for marriage. So they get involved in pornography or become sexually active in some way.
- Some kids are so desperate for friends they compromise and settle for quick, shallow friendships with others who aren't a

good influence on them rather than building a better friendship with someone else.

Can you think of other ways people compromise and take short-cuts, settling for something wrong or lesser now instead of waiting for the better or right thing later?

The Bible is full of stories of people who satisfied their urges instead of holding out for the greater reward. David's treatment of Bathsheba is an example of that. Later, he regretted horribly what he had done. He wrote Psalm 51 as a result . . . and the pain from his bad decision haunted him and his family for the rest of his life.

And there are also stories of others who did it right. Like Joseph, who resisted the temptation of Potiphar's wife. If he hadn't, he may have never been in a position to rule Egypt as he did.

Sometimes, we have to delay that urge we have for instant gratification and wait for something that is far better: God's plan and his timing.

When Esau traded his birthright for a bowl of stew, that was a slap in the face to his dad, wasn't it? His dad had prepared so much for Esau—yet Esau tossed it away for a bowl of grub. How do you think God feels when he tells us to wait for things, and we rush ahead and trade what he offers for something of much less value . . . just so we can have it now?

Summing It Up

Waiting for something we want *now* takes self-control and patience. The Holy Spirit can help us with those, if we ask him. Those are two of his specialties.

> But the fruit of the Spirit is love, joy, peace, **patience**, kindness, goodness, faithfulness, gentleness, **self-control**; against such things there is no law. (Gal. 5:22–23 ESV, emphasis added)

Assuming one or more of your kids disqualified themselves for the IOU snack shopping spree, we have another chance for them to learn the principle of delayed gratification. You'll give each of the kids their special $5 bill—whether they ate snacks earlier or not. Hopefully all of them will save that money, and you can reinforce the principle on that date you wrote on the margin.

I have a $5 bill for each of you. And you'll notice I wrote a little note in the margin. You can spend this $5 anytime you want. It's yours. But if you wait until after (fill in a date at least 2–3 months away), you can give it back to me and I'll give you $10 (or $20 . . . whatever you can afford) for it. It must be this exact $5 bill though, not a different one.

It will take some patience and self-control, but I want you to learn that good things come to those who wait. And that isn't just the case with this money but especially with the truth from God's Word. For example, if God tells us to wait for sex—and he does—then trust him. You won't regret it. Esau lived with regret the rest of his life for his bad decision . . . for his inability to wait. I don't want that happening to you.

For the moment all discipline seems painful rather than pleasant, but later it yields the peaceful fruit of righteousness to those who have been trained by it.

Therefore lift your drooping hands and strengthen your weak knees, and make straight paths for your feet, so that what is lame may not be put out of joint but rather be healed. Strive for peace with everyone, and for the holiness without which no one will see the Lord. See to it that no one fails to obtain the grace of God; that no "root of bitterness" springs up and causes trouble, and by it many become defiled; that no one is sexually immoral or unholy like Esau, who sold his birthright for a single meal. For you know that afterward, when he desired to inherit the blessing, he was rejected, for he found no chance to repent, though he sought it with tears. (Heb. 12:11–17 ESV)

God has a plan . . . and it is good. Will you trust him enough to do it his way? That means you'll need to wait for some things. But the wait is always worth it in the end.

Therefore, since we are surrounded by so great a cloud of witnesses, let us also lay aside every weight, and sin which clings so closely, and let us run with endurance the race that is set before us, looking to Jesus, the founder and perfecter of our faith, who for the joy that was set before him endured the cross, despising the shame, and is seated at the right hand of the throne of God. (vv. 1–2 ESV)

You may want to mark the maturity date of the $5 bills on your calendar so you can check with the kids at that time. If they didn't spend the money . . . make a big deal of that. Reinforce this lesson at that time—and remind them to apply that same discipline to obeying God's Word and his timing for everything, including sex.

Tim Shoemaker is the author of more than twenty books and is a popular speaker at conferences and schools around the country. He is a regular contributor to Focus on the Family *Clubhouse* and *Clubhouse Jr.* magazines. Tim loves writing contemporary novels for youth filled with mystery, adventure, and suspense, such as award-winning *Easy Target, Escape from the Everglades*, and the rest of the High Water series. His contemporary suspense novel *Code of Silence* was named in the "Top Ten Crime Novels for Youth" by *Booklist*.

Happily married for more than forty years, Tim lives in Illinois and still loves working with youth.